D1436892

FADO
PORTUGUÊS
Songs from the soul of Portugal

FADO
PORTUGUÊS
Songs from the soul of Portugal

A COLLECTION OF POPULAR PORTUGUESE FADOS
Compiled and edited by Donald Cohen
Translations by Donald Cohen and David Martins

Music arranged for voice and guitar

WISE PUBLICATIONS
part of The Music Sales Group
London/New York/Paris/Sydney/Copenhagen/Berlin/Madrid/Tokyo

This book is lovingly dedicated to Barbara, Shelley, Greg, Darryl, Doriena, Adrienne, Oliver and to all of the *fadistas* and *guitarristas* who have given me so many hours of pleasure over the years.

Exclusive Distributors:

Music Sales Limited
8/9 Frith Street, London W1D 3JB, England.

Music Sales Corporation
257 Park Avenue South, New York, NY10010, United States of America.

Music Sales Pty Limited
120 Rothschild Avenue, Rosebery, NSW 2018, Australia.

© Copyright 2003 Wise Publications, a division of Music Sales Limited.

Unauthorised reproduction of any part of this publication by any means including photocopying is an infringement of copyright.

Limp Edition:
Order No. AM964150
ISBN: 0-7119-8229-5

Cased Edition:
Order No. AM84377
ISBN: 0-7119-2609-3

Music arranged by Donald Cohen
Music processed by Paul Ewers Music Design
English translations by David Martins and Donald Cohen
Book design by Chloë Alexander

 Images on pages 8, 10, 22, 37, 38, 50, 62, 66, 92, 116 & 137 are the property of Casa do Fado e da Guitarra Portuguesa.

All other photographs courtesy of AA World Travel Library, Arquivo de Fotografia de Lisboa, Daniel Blaufuks, Homem Cardoso & Luis Catarino – AIC, Donald Cohen, Sue Cunningham, Jon Lusk/Redferns, Rick Perry, Portuguese National Tourist Office, Celeste Rodrigues, Rasa Sekulovic and Valentim de Carvalho.

Every effort has been made to trace the copyright holders of the photographs in this book but one or two were unreachable. We would be grateful if the photographers concerned would contact us.

Printed in Malta by Interprint Limited.

◀ An early photo of an Amália Rodrigues performance at a typical *fado* club.

Front cover An early depiction of an impromptu street performance in one of the old *bairros* (districts) of Lisbon. Such performances were quite common in the early part of the last century and could be experienced, occasionally up until the 1970s.

CONTENTS

ACKNOWLEDGEMENTS

FOR THEIR ASSISTANCE I would like to thank my friends the *fadistas* and *fado* musicians Celeste Rodrigues, Carlos do Carmo, Rodrigo, João Pestana Dias, José Elmiro Nunes, Cidália Maria, Helio Beirão and the late Aniceto Batista.

Also Veronica Paine and Inés Penalva of Velentim de Carvalho Records, Paul Vernon, author and true authority on *fado*, Tom Schnabel, LA radio host and world music expert, California *fadista* Aurelio Oliveira, Emanuel Oliveira, Rick Perry, California Portuguese radio host Tito Rebelo, Maria Bing, Gloria do Mello of TAP Airlines, Alberto Veloso of King Holidays USA, Sra. Elena Silva, Ursula Mactissel, Rita Varela Silva, professor Ricardo Sternberg, Chairman of the Department of Brazilian and Portuguese at the University of Toronto, filmmaker Bruno da Almeida, producer of the definitive film documentary on the life and career of Amália Rodrigues, Alexandra Baltazar of the Portuguese National Tourist Office, my good friend Professor Ed Cray of the University of Southern California, and the always amiable and supportive the Hon. Edmundo Mecedo, Consul of Portugal in Los Angeles.

A particular thanks is owed to my dear friend Margrit Klein, formerly of TAP Portuguese Airlines, and also to dear friends George and Mary Sousa who first guided me into the world of *fado* in Northern California while filling me with the finest Portuguese wines and cuisine. A posthumous vote of appreciation is owed to my brother, the late Martin Cohen, attorney, horticulturist and wine connoisseur, for his encouragement of this project.

A truly special expression of praise and gratitude is owed for the generous doses of his vast knowledge of Portuguese language and culture provided by my dear friend UCLA professor emeritus Eduardo Mayone Dias, a Portuguese authority and author in his own right. His assistance with the translations and proof reading of the entire text is greatly appreciated.

For their special assistance and cooperation in the publication of this book, I would particularly like to thank the very creative Chloë Alexander, as well as Sarah Bacon, Sarah Holcroft, Lucy Holliday, Tom Fleming and Julia Robinson. My gratitude, also to Roger Eaglestone, whose editing and coordinating skills contributed so much to the book's completion, and, last but not least, a special note of thanks to the head of Wise Publications/Music Sales Ltd., Robert Wise, who first suggested the writing of this book and who was ultimately responsible for its publication.

Finally, I owe a great debt to my life partner and dearest friend, my wife Barbara, who patiently endured endless telephone calls, faxes, e-mails and conferences, often at indecent hours of the night, as well as an insane work schedule.

I am convinced that I have omitted a number of people whose help should have been recognised and that I will awaken from sleep the night after publication with their names emblazoned before me. So I ask their forgiveness at this time. In spite of the best efforts of all of the above individuals, certain errors are bound to have inserted themselves into the manuscript, and for these I, alone, am responsible.

Donald Cohen

▼ A modern Lisbon billboard showing Amália Rodrigues, the undisputed Queen of the *fado*.

ALTHOUGH *FADO* as it is known today is no more than, perhaps, 200 years old, the musical and lyrical traditions that led to its creation go as far back, possibly, as the creation of the Portuguese nation itself.

At the time when Portugal was founded in 1143, there existed a number of highly stylised ballad forms. Among these were the *Chanso*, a noble song sung by the aristocracy, the *Sirventês*, sung by soldiers, the *Plang*, a form of lament, the *Cantiga de Amigo*, sung by a woman to a man, and the *Cantiga de Amor*, sung by a man to a woman. There was also a song/poem of satirical expression called the *Cantiga de Escárneo* or *Cantiga de Mal-dizer* (Song Of Mockery or Song Of Speaking Ill [of someone]).

Some of these forms developed largely as the result of the tradition of Provençal poetry introduced into Portugal by the knights and minstrels of Henry of Burgundy, the father of Portugal's first king, Afonso Henriques. Contributing to its unique character is the fact that, after more than eight centuries, the present-day *fado* still preserves, within itself, substantial and visible elements of these early musical forms.

Other influences which contributed to the development of *fado* are those of the Moors and Jews who played such a large role in Portugal's early history. Both of these groups had specific forms of poems and ballads, extremely popular, which entered the culture, both in their form and content.

Last of the factors which contributed to the *fado's* development was the Portuguese nation's monumental maritime explorations and the subsequent creation of the Portuguese empire. The Portuguese sailors, explorers and colonisers who voyaged to the East, to Africa, and to the New World brought back foreign musical forms and ideas which some musicologists feel contributed to the evolution of the Lisbon *fado*.

There are, to be sure, two other forms of *fado*. The first, the Coimbra *fado*, named for the ancient university town in the centre of Portugal, was created by the students at that ancient Portuguese seat of learning. It is, in fact, still sung by them, and by the doctors and lawyers who represent the alumni, to this day. The other is the *fado* of Porto, Portugal's second largest city, which differs from Lisbon *fado* only in subtle distinctions, of interest only to *fado* musicians and *fadistas* (singers of *fado*). It is, however, the Lisbon *fado* with which the rest of the world has become most familiar.

The development of the *fado* as we know it (the word is derived from the Latin *fatum*, meaning 'fate') took place from the late 18th Century in several of the oldest sections of Lisbon: the Alfama, Mouraria, Bairro Alto and Madragoa districts.

Fado is traditionally accompanied by one or two Portuguese guitars and the classic six-string Spanish guitar. In Portugal, the latter instrument is called the 'Portuguese viola', which can sometimes cause considerable confusion among non-Portuguese. The Portuguese guitar is a rather unique instrument, somewhat resembling a mandolin in appearance, from which six double strings serve to emit a unique, rich and hauntingly beautiful sound. At the top of the neck the 12 screws which hold the strings are arranged on a fan-shaped tuning head which is often called the Portuguese equivalent of a 'turkey's tail'. *Fado* is usually performed in small, intimate cafés called *adegas típicas* or *casas do fado* which are almost always located in the oldest districts of Lisbon, the Alfama, the Bairro Alto and Madragoa.

Female *fadistas* will frequently appear wearing a black shawl which is traditionally worn in mourning for the death of the best known and most revered of early performers of *fado*, the 19th Century Gypsy Maria Severa. It was as a result of her tempestuous and notorious affair with the noble Count de Vimioso that *fado*, originally music of the streets and brothels, gained respectability and entered the homes of the upper classes and even of the aristocracy.

In order to understand what the songs themselves are about, it is necessary to become familiar with the Portuguese word *saudade*. Although the word has the same origin as the Italian *solita* or the Spanish *soledad* which are translated as 'loneliness', *saudade* has a much broader, and exclusively Portuguese meaning which is quite untranslatable. The closest we can come is a sentiment of sad, nostalgic memory or yearning. Love and longing for the past are certainly a part of any definition. The term *saudade* is to be found in innumerable *fados* while *saudade* itself is the subject of a great number of them.

Equally popular as a subject of *fado* is the city of Lisbon itself, which, as a result, is probably the subject of more songs than any city in the world – more than Paris or even Buenos Aires. Virtually every other song is about Lisbon or one of its *bairros* (districts). There are, of course, a great many songs about love, often unrequited, parting and separation, and mothers and fathers, (the Portuguese are by nature profoundly sentimental). Anything can be the subject of a *fado*. For example, one very popular song was written complaining about the price of *bacalhao* (codfish), a Portuguese staple. A final and very frequent subject of *fado* is the *fado* itself. There are literally hundreds of songs about why one sings *fado*, who sings it and to whom it should be sung.

▼ An early photo of Tristão da Silva, one of the finest *fadistas* (*fado* singers) of the mid-20th Century, beginning in the 1940s accompanied by a Portuguese guitar and two Portuguese violas (Spanish guitars).

There are three basic types of traditional Lisbon *fado*. These are the *fado Menor* (minor *fado*), *fado Corrido* (running *fado*), and the *fado Mouraria*, the last being named for one of the ancient districts of Lisbon. The latter two forms are very similar, and vary, actually, only in very subtle differences in the traditional, highly stylised, Portuguese guitar accompaniment used for each.

The purest form of traditional *fado*, in terms of subject matter, is termed *fado castiço*. The word *castiço*, from the same Latin root as 'caste' means the 'true' or 'pure' *fado* and refers to a particular class of songs, the lyrics of which speak of the nobility and noble pursuits: of courtly love, bullfighting, and, as previously mentioned, of *fado* itself. This certainly was one of *fado's* earliest forms.

The Portuguese are fond of saying that the previously described three types of *fado* – *Menor, Corrido and Mouraria* – are the only traditional forms of *fado*. That is only partially true. Over many generations melodic variations on the traditional *fados* have evolved, usually created by prominent singers or guitarists. These are often named for their creators (*fado Marceneiro, fado Pedro Rodrigues, fado Vianinha),* sometimes for famous historical figures

(*fado Pombalinho*), and sometimes, as in *fado Triplicado* or *fado Seixal* , named for the number of lines of verse for which they were created. These variations themselves became stylised and the bases for a larger body of *fados* in that the melodies have, in themselves, become traditional and new lyrics are continually created and sung to them.

Early in this century, and perhaps even earlier, singers employed to perform in the *fado* houses, desperate for new material, began to hire music and literature professors, even doctors and lawyers, to create new ballads which were set to the old traditional melodies described above. At some point these writers began to compose melodies of their own so that a further development over the last century has been that of a more popular form of *fado*, sometimes referred to as *fado musicado* or *fado moderno*. These *fados*, should they remain popular and maintain a place in the repertoires of prominent *fadistas*, are eventually referred to as 'classic' *fados* although they are not traditional in form.

There are, however, a great many songs that have achieved wide popularity over the years among both *fadistas* and lovers of *fado* but which fall within a grey area. These are sometimes the subjects of dispute as to whether they should be considered *fado* or merely *canção* (popular songs). To add to the confusion some contemporary writers will refer to some of the more modern compositions as '*fado canção*'. And yet, on another level, this entire muddle makes sense since, as *fado* is a living art form, it is constantly changing and such change inevitably invites controversy.

A brief comment is in order about another interesting institution associated with the *fado*. This is a form of amateur *fado* event referred to as *fado vadio* (vagrant's or vagabond's *fado*). This is an amateur performance in a number of *fado* houses in which various members of the audience get up to perform, and I have seen the participants vary from the young to the very old of both sexes. In some of the *fado* houses such performances follow the end of the professional presentation, while in some of the smaller houses *fado vadio* represents the entire evening's entertainment.

After the death of long time dictator António Salazar in 1970 and Portugal's bloodless 'Revolution' of 25 April 1974, some Portuguese, particularly among the younger generation, rejected *fado* as being a reflection of the reactionary and repressive past. During this period, the type of amateur performance described above was rarely heard.

The last two decades, however, have seen a great resurgence of interest in *fado*, both in its traditional form and in adapting and reinterpreting *fado* to reflect the modern Portugal. The young Portuguese have come to realise that they love the music and that it is too integral a part of Portuguese culture to be ignored.

The most difficult task in completing this collection was in choosing which of the innumerable beautiful *fados* to include and which to omit. The selection was made on the basis of several criteria. Among these was the song's popularity among the singers themselves, i.e. how frequently it was recorded, as well as whether it represented a particular type of *fado*. Sometimes we felt that the lyrics were of particular interest. Finally, of course, we looked to the beauty of its melody. In the end the selection was, by its very nature, entirely subjective. There are those who will question our choices and they will, indeed, be correct… just as we were.

In the following collection we have attempted to present a comprehensive and varied sampling of some of the most popular Lisbon *fados* and have included a Coimbra *fado* and fine examples of the three traditional *fado* forms, *fado Menor, fado Corrido and fado Mouraria*. The only thing more satisfying than playing and singing these exciting and often haunting melodies would be to find oneself seated in a colourful old *adega típica* in Lisbon, a glass of fine Portuguese wine on the table before you, enjoying their performance by some of the great artists of the *fado*.

Boa Sorte! (Good luck!)

LISBOA ANTIGA

Ancient Lisbon

Raul Portela / José Galhardo / Amadeu dos Santos

ALTHOUGH IT IS IMPOSSIBLE to select any particular *fado* as the most popular among Portuguese, this song is unquestionably the most popular *fado* as far as non-Portuguese are concerned. Traditionally speaking, '*Lisboa Antiga*' and the song following it are not *fados* at all. Originally Portuguese popular hits, they have been accepted as belonging within the *fado* genre by virtue of their association with the greatest of the exponents of *fado* in the 20th Century, Amália Rodrigues. Introduced by Amália to world-wide audiences early in her career, it is one of a number of *fados* that became international hits. The refrain is often heard as instrumental 'background' music in restaurants and hotels in America and on the Continent. '*Lisboa Antiga*' is the one song that many foreign tourists will request upon first visiting a *fado* house in Lisbon. Among Portuguese it is universally known and loved and is widely sung and recorded by *fadistas* even today.

The career of Amália Rodrigues, who passed away in 1999, spanned a period of over 50 years, during which she became not only a world-class artist but a universally acclaimed symbol of Portuguese vocal and creative arts. Singers, musicians and other artists covering the spectrum of creative endeavour from all over the world have sung her praise. She was the undisputed Queen of the *Fado* and her renderings of this ancient song form renewed it, transcended its national character and gave it universal appeal.

Born in 1920, she and her sister, Celeste, another eminent *fadista,* came from a poor family and grew up in the Alcântara, one of the oldest, poorest, but musically rich sections of Lisbon. Amália was discovered selling oranges in the streets and along the docks of Lisbon. Beginning her professional career at the age of 15, Amália had become a star by 1940. Her enormously rich voice and uniquely recognisable style reached their prime in the 1950s and continued thereafter for more than three decades.

So profoundly important a representative of Portuguese culture was she considered that, when she died in October 1999, the Portuguese government declared three days of national mourning and flags were flown at half-mast. The President of Portugal was chief mourner at the singer's state funeral and crowds of people could be seen weeping in the streets throughout Lisbon. The first three *fados* in this collection are among the songs that Amália Rodrigues introduced to world-wide audiences during the course of her spectacular career.

The word '*réis*' refers to a coin in circulation during Portugal's royal period. The term '*esperas*' – literally 'to wait for' or 'delay' – describes an old bullfighting tradition – more fully termed *esperas de gado.* While the bulls were run through the streets on their way to the arena – a custom which still takes place each year in several bullfight-loving countries (the most famous event taking place in Pamplona, Spain) – local fans hold up the start of the formal bullfight in the ring by diverting one of the bulls in order to fight it in the streets. Traditional *fado* was often concerned with themes of the nobility and the bullring.

This song is typical of a large number of *fados* that portray Lisbon as a woman, frequently a young girl, often a princess. The Tagus River (*Tejo,* in Portuguese), one of the two great rivers of Portugal, reaches the Atlantic at Lisbon. It is both directly and by allusion a popular topic of *fado,* as are its sailors, ferrymen and even its fishmongers. Note that Amália sings only the first verse on her recording.

◄ Amália Rodrigues the undisputed Queen of the *fado*. Amália was so revered by the Portuguese and so influential in introducing *fado* to world audiences she was designated a Portuguese 'national treasure'.

LISBOA ANTIGA

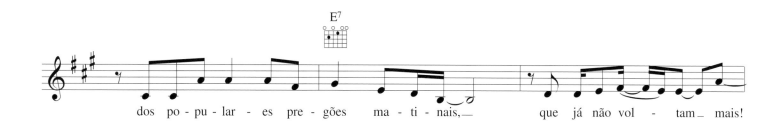

dos po - pu - lar - es pre - gões ma - ti - nais,— que já não vol - tam— mais!

1. Am | **Free time** | **2.** A
N.C.

———— Lis - bo - a vel - ha ci mais!

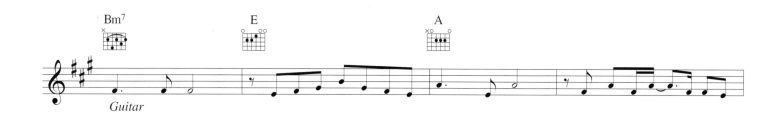

Bm7 E A

Guitar

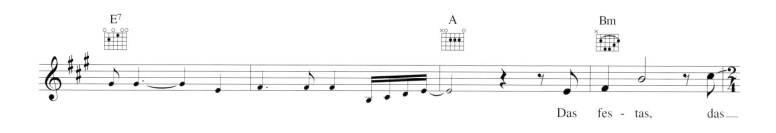

E7 A Bm

Das fes - tas, das—

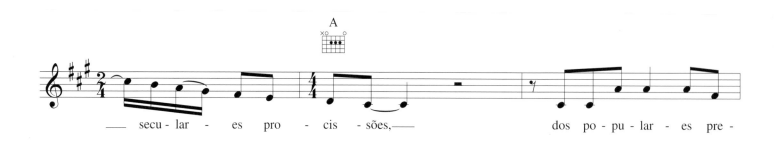

A

—— secu - lar - es pro - cis - sões,— dos po - pu - lar - es pre -

E7 A E7 A

- gões ma - ti - nais,— que já não vol - tam— mais!——

1 Lisboa, velha cidade
   Cheia de encanto e beleza,
   Sempre formosa,
   A sorrir
   E ao vestir
   Sempre airosa.
   O branco véu da saudade
   Cobre o teu rosto, linda princesa.

   Refrain
   Olhai, senhores,
   Esta Lisboa d'outras eras,
   Dos cinco Réis, das esperas
   E das touradas reais;
   Das festas,
   Das seculares procissões,
   Dos populares pregões matinais
   Que já não voltam mais !

2 Lisboa, de ouro e de prata,
   Outra mais linda não vejo,
   Eternamente
   A brincar
   E a cantar
   De contente.
   O teu semblante se retrato
   No azul cristalino do Tejo.

   Refrain

Lisbon, old city
Vision of enchantment and beauty
With her lovely smile,
Clothed in dignity
The white veil of *saudade* covers your face,
Beautiful Princess

Refrain
Look! it is the Lisbon of other eras,
Of the five *réis*, the *esperas*
And of the royal bullfights;
The festivals, the age-old processions,
The cries of the street vendors in the mornings
That will never return again

Lisbon, city of gold and silver
I have never seen another more beautiful;
Eternally playful and joyfully singing,
You appear as a portrait
In the crystalline blue of the Tagus

Refrain

*Lisbon, old city
Vision of enchantment and
beauty*

COIMBRA

José Galhardo / Raul Ferrão

THIS *FADO*, as the one preceding it, is one of the songs made internationally famous by Amália Rodrigues. In fact, it was her first international hit, recorded in a live performance at the famous Olympia Theatre in Paris in 1951. Named for the picturesque, ancient city in the centre of Portugal, the song, first a big hit in Europe in a French version, '*Avril Au Portugal*', achieved a wide popularity in an English version under the title 'April In Portugal'. The writers of this song were two of Portugal's most illustrious poets and composers, Jose Galhardo and Raul Ferrão, both of whom will be discussed later in this book. However, one curious fact emerges regarding '*Coimbra*'. Ferrão had actually created this work in 1939, but, as he was writing reviews and shows, and had no current work in which to place it, the song sat in his drawer until it finally appeared in 1947 in the Portuguese film *Capas Negras* (Black Capes), about the students at the University of Coimbra. At that time the song had little success until three years later when Amália Rodrigues picked it up for her next international tour and which ultimately included the above-described monumental recording at the Olympia.

Although the song is about Coimbra, its famed university, founded in the Middle Ages, and its students, this song is not a true Coimbra *fado*. Those songs, traditionally created by the students or the doctors and lawyers making up the faculty and alumni, are entirely different, both in their style and structure.

The Coimbra *fado* is usually a languorously slow, romantic and sentimental poem set to music; the subject of these ballads are typically feelings of *saudade* for the University, one's beloved, or for the *fado* itself. An example of a true Coimbra *fado* is presented under the title *'Fado Hilário'*, later in this collection. Note the continual use of simile throughout. Metaphor, simile and the use of symbolism are consistently present in the romantic, evocative and often tragic themes that pervade *fado*.

The word *'Choupal'* in the first line of the song, which translates as 'poplar grove' refers to a famous landmark of Coimbra, a wide poplar tree-lined walkway which is often mentioned in sentimental ballads and *fados* about the city.

The allusion to an '*Inês*' in the first verse is a reference to one of the most popular and tragic figures in Portuguese history. Inês de Castro was a beautiful young Castilian noblewoman, a lady-in-waiting to the wife of Dom Pedro, son of the Portuguese king, Alfonso IV.

Having wed only for reasons of state, Dom Pedro fell in love with Inês and, upon the death of his wife, knowing that his father would oppose his marriage to a Spaniard for political reasons, he secretly married her, keeping her hidden in a *quinta* (manor house) in Coimbra. Three children were born to the couple. Several courtiers, fearing Spanish interference in Portuguese royal affairs, informed the king of the marriage and persuaded him to have Inês murdered in Coimbra in 1355.

Dom Pedro had his revenge when he ascended the throne. After personally executing the two of the trio of murderers he could find, he had his beloved's body brought from her tomb in state. Dressing her in royal robes and a crown, he had her seated on the throne next to him and forced the courtiers to kiss her pallid hand. Pedro ordered that she be placed in a tomb of his own design and, upon his death, was, by his command, positioned facing her, so that, on the Day of Judgement, their first sight upon opening their eyes would be of each other. The tragic tale of Portugal's Romeo and Juliet is well known and loved by all Portuguese, young and old.

▶ A later photo of Amália Rodrigues taken during a concert in Southern California

COIMBRA

Co - im - bra é u-ma li - ção, de son - ho e tra - di - ção;

O len -te é u-ma can - ção, e a lu - a a Fa -cul - dade;

O liv -ro e u-ma mul - her, só pas -sa quem sou - ber... E a-

To Coda ⊕ Am

- pren -de -se a di - zer: *Sau - dade!* 1.Co o -

- im - bra do Chou - pal, A - in - da és ca - pi - tal do a -

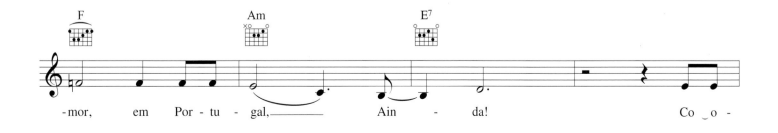

-mor, em Por - tu - gal, Ain - da! Co o -

-im - bra, onde u - ma vez, com lá - grim - as, se fez, a his-

-to - ri - a des-sa In - ês_____ tão_____ lin - da!_____ 2.Co _ o - im-

- bra das can - - - ções tã - o mei - gas que nos pões os_____

_____ nos - sos _____ cor - a - ções_____ a nu!_____ O Co-

-im - bra dos dou - tor - es, Pa - ra nós, os teus_____ can - tor - es, a

Fon - te dos A - mor - es és tu! _____ Co-

D.%. al Coda

⊕ *Coda*

- dade!   *Guitar*

20

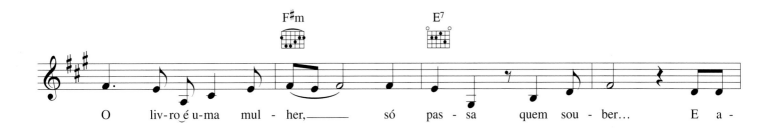

O liv-ro é u-ma mul - her,_____ só pas - sa quem sou - ber... E a-

Free time

- pren - de - se a di - zer:_____ *Sau - - - dade!*

1 Coimbra do Choupal,
   Ainda és capital
   Do amor, em Portugal,
   Ainda !
   Coimbra, onde uma vez,
   Com lágrimas, se fez
   A história dessa Inês
   Tão linda!

2 Coimbra das canções
   Tão meigas
   Que nos pões
   Os nossos corações
   A nu !
   Coimbra dos doutores,
   Para nós, os teus cantores,
   A Fonte dos Amores
   És tu !

   Refrain
   Coimbra é uma lição
   De sonho e tradição;
   O lente é uma canção
   E a lua a Faculdade;
   O livro é uma mulher;
   Só passa quem souber…
   E aprende-se a dizer:
   Saudade!

Coimbra of the Poplar Grove
You are still the capital
Of love, in Portugal,
Even now
Coimbra, where once,
With tears, was written
The story of that *Inês*
So lovely

Coimbra of the songs
So tender
That our hearts
You bare,
Coimbra of the scholars,
Who for us are your singers,
The Fountain of Love
Is you!

Refrain
Coimbra is a lesson
Of dream and tradition
A song is the teacher,
The moon, the faculty,
A book is a woman…
Only he passes who knows…
And learns to say:
Saudade !

AI, MOURARIA

Oh, Mouraria

Frederico Valério / Amadeu do Vale

THE MOURARIA is one of the oldest *bairros*, or districts, of Lisbon. The word 'Mouraria' comes from the word '*Mouro*', or Moor, as this district began as a Moorish enclave. It is also famous in *fado* lore for two reasons:

First, because it was one of the areas where, in the earliest days, many taverns and brothels were located. It was in this colourful, but somewhat disreputable, part of the city and in these low-class meeting places that the *fado* was first created and nurtured. Second, because it was in the Mouraria that Maria Severa, nicknamed A Severa (see Introduction), was born and flourished. A Severa was considered the finest and most celebrated of the *fadistas* in the 19th Century.

By virtue of the above, as well as because of its origins and early history, the Mouraria was one of the most culturally rich districts in Lisbon. It is also the subject of a great deal of nostalgia because, in the mid-20th Century, before the forces of historical preservation had found their voice in Portugal, developers were allowed to 'redevelop' most of the district, tearing down many of the historical and colourful old buildings.

There were a great many *fados* written about the Mouraria in the early days, as well as a number of *fados* created to mourn its fate, including one popular song starkly entitled 'They Have Murdered The Mouraria'. Note, once again, the reference to 'processions passing' in the refrain. The descriptions are referring to the various popular as well as religious processions that normally took place on saint's days, feast days, and the birthdays, weddings, etc. of the aristocracy. These were so much a part of the life of old Lisbon, particularly in the ancient districts of Mouraria, Alfama, Bairro Alto and Madragoa, that no description of these sites seems adequate without them.

'*Ai, Mouraria*' is the third of the quartet of songs in this collection that is identified with Amália Rodrigues. She first recorded it in Rio de Janeiro in 1945. The song is one of love betrayed but eternal and, although not traditional, it remains a true classic.

▼ Blind street singer in the ancient Mouraria district. Blind beggars, receiving no government support, were given the governmental privilege of playing and singing *fado* on the streets to earn a few escudos

The song is one of love betrayed but eternal and, although not traditional, it remains a true classic

AI, MOURARIA

♩= 104
Free time
a tempo
A
F
E7
1. Ai, Mou - ra - ri - - - a, de vel - ha ru - a da
(Verse 2 see block lyric)
Am
G
Pal - ma, on - de eu um di - a
a tempo
G7
C
Am
E7
dei - xei pre - sa a min - - - ha al - ma. Por ter pas -
2° (A7)
2° (Dm)
Am
E7
- sa - - - do mes - mo ao la - do cer - to fa - dis - ta
2° (E7)
Dm6
Dm/F
de côr mo - re - na, bo - ca pe - que - na, ol - har tro -
1.
2.
Free time ad lib.
- cis - ta. 2. Ai, Mou - ra - - i - go.

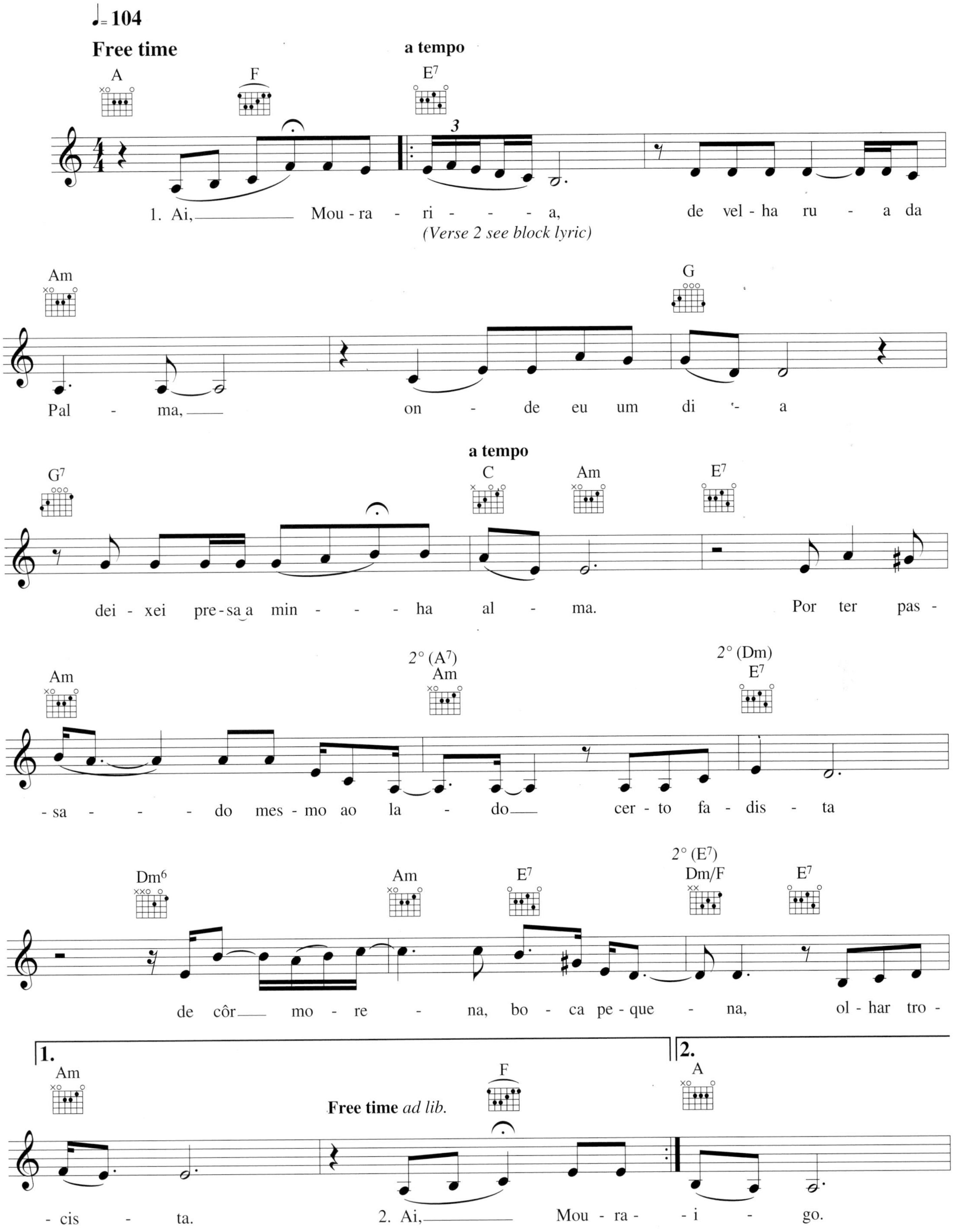

Free time   F#7   a tempo   E7

Ai,___ Mou-ra - ri - a   dos rou-xi - nois___ nos be - ir -

A   C#7

- ais,   dos ves - ti - dos côr de___ ro-sa,_____ dos pre-gões___

D   E♭dim   A   F#7

___ tra - di - cion - ais.___   Ai,_____ Mou-ra -

E7   A

- ri - a   das pro - cis - sões___ a pas - sar,___

B7   E7

da Se - ve - ra, a voz sau - do - sa   na gui - tar - ra a so - lu -

A   Free time   F#7   a tempo   E7

Guitar

- çar.

A

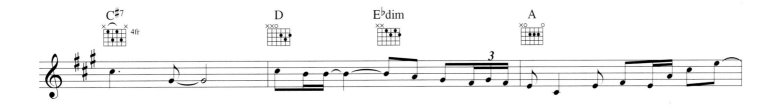

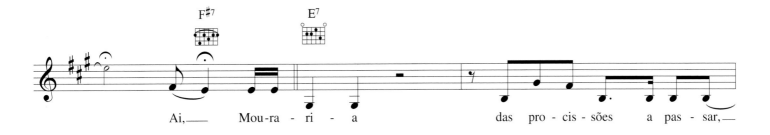

Ai,___ Mou-ra - ri - a das pro - cis - sões a pas - sar,___

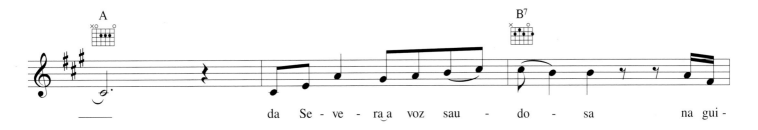

___ da Se - ve - ra_a voz sau - do - sa na gui-

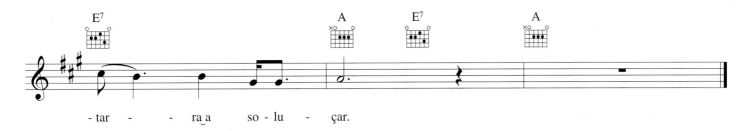

- tar - - ra_a so - lu - çar.

1 Ai, Mouraria, da velha rua da Palma,
 Onde eu um dia deixei presa a minha alma
 Por ter passado mesmo ao lado certo fadista
 De côr morena, boca pequena, olhar trocista

2 Ai, Mouraria, do homem do meu encanto
 Que me mentia mas que eu adorava tanto.
 Amor que o vento como um lamento levou consigo
 Mas que ainda agora e a toda a hora trago comigo

Refrain
Ai, Mouraria dos rouxinois nos beirais
Dos vestidos côr de rosa, dos pregões tradicionais.
Ai, Mouraria das procissões a passar,
Da Severa, a voz saudosa na guitarra a soluçar } *Repeat*

Oh Mouraria of the old Palm Street
Where one day I lost my soul
As there passed by a certain *fadista*
With dark skin, a small mouth, and mocking eyes

Oh Mouraria of the man who charmed me
And lied to me, but whom I loved so much
A love that the wind, like a lament, swept away
That, still now, and every single day I carry with me

Refrain
Oh, Mouraria of the nightingales on the rooftops
Of the pink dresses, of the traditional street vendors
Oh, Mouraria of the processions passing by
Of Severa, a yearning voice in the sobbing guitar

*Oh, Mouraria of the nightingales
on the rooftops
    Of the pink dresses, of the
traditional street vendors
    Oh, Mouraria of the processions
        passing by
    Of Severa, a yearning voice
in the sobbing guitar*

POR MORRER UMA ANDORINHA
For The Death Of A Swallow

Joaquim Frederico de Brito / Francisco Viana / Américo dos Santos

THIS IS AN example of a modern *fado*, one particularly identified with Carlos do Carmo, an enormously popular singer and one of the foremost *fadistas* of the last half century.

Carlos Manuel de Ascenção Almeida is the birth name of Carlos do Carmo, born in Lisbon in either 1939 or 1941, the sources here are conflicting. He is the son of Lucila do Carmo, one of the great interpreters of *fado* during the mid-century era, and therefore took her name when he began to perform.

The young Carlos was sent to Switzerland for his education, engaging in the study of languages and hotel management. During that time of his life his musical tastes were more inclined chiefly toward Brazilian *bosso-nova*, as well as the vocal renderings of singers such as Frank Sinatra and Jacques Brel.

Upon his return to Portugal, the young Carlos, then still Almeida, was soon obliged, with the death of his father, to undertake the management of the family owned *adega típica*, 'O Faia', one of Lisbon's most popular *fado* clubs. At the increasing insistence of his friends and patrons, Do Carmo began to perform in public. After deciding to become a *fadista* he attempted, for a time, to reconcile the careers of singer and club manager, but as his popularity increased, this effort was clearly unsuccessful. Do Carmo began his career in 1963 and in the following 35 years recorded prolifically, with enormous success. Many of the songs that he introduced, such as the one following as well as '*Meu Bairro Alto*', '*Gaivota*', '*Canoas do Tejo*', '*Os Putos*', '*Um Homem Na Cidade*' and others, have become great classics.

He is one of the few *fadistas* that, like Amália, was able to establish an international following. His compelling voice and elegant style, as well as the skillful manner in which he has managed his career has led him to sing in such prestigious venues as the Olympia in Paris and opera houses and concert halls throughout Europe, North and South America, Asia, India, and Africa. Do Carmo, in addition to his extensive touring, recently hosted a series featuring *fado* on Portuguese television.

Although extremely skilled in the rendering of traditional *fado*, Carlos do Carmo is representative of the modern *fadistas* who consistently perform and record newly adapted and rearranged early poems and ballads while also promoting newly written *fados* by contemporary composers. These songs, often distinguished from traditional *fado* by being termed *fado musicado* or even *fado canção* (*fado* song), do not necessarily fit into the structures of traditional *fado*. The newer *fados* frequently explore more contemporary themes and utilise a more modern approach, both as to composition and arrangement. Band or orchestral instruments are sometimes used to accompany modern interpreters of *fado* in their recordings.

One of the composers of '*Por Morrer Uma Andorinha*', Frederico de Brito, was a brilliant poet and an extremely prolific composer of beautiful *fados*. When, during the earlier part of this century, this new form of *fado* appeared, it created a great deal of controversy. Traditionalists decried the use of refrains, different types of melody and non-traditional themes, and complained it was no longer '*castiço*', i.e. 'the real thing'. In reply, de Brito penned the following verse of *fado* that expressed his views on the matter:

You speak to me of *fado castiço*?
Leave that aside!
Here is only one kind (of *fado*)
And that's enough!
A melody that holds us,
However much they may have changed it.
Lively or sad,
With refrain or without, it is always *Fado*!

◄ A young Carlos do Carmo performing at his *fado* club 'O Faia'

Carlos do Carmo, an enormously popular singer and one of the foremost fadistas *of the last half century*

POR MORRER UMA ANDORINHA

♩= 104

Harp

cont. sim.

1. Se dei - xas - - te de ser min - ha,
(Verse 2 see block lyric)

não dei - xei de ser quem e - ra.   Por— mor-rer u - ma an-dor-in-ha

não——— a - ca-ba a Pri-ma - ve - ra.   Por— mor-rer u - ma an-dor-

-in - ha   não a - ca - ba a Pri - ma - ve - ra.—

3. Eu— já es - ta - va ha-bi - tua - do   a— que não— fosses— sin -

30

-ce-ra por is-so não fi-co á es-pe-ra

du-ma il-usão que não tin-ha. Se sei-xas-te de ser

min-ha, não dei-xei de ser quem e-ra.

Se dei-xas-te de ser min-ha, não dei-xei de ser quem e-ra.

4. Vi-vo a vi-da co-mo dan-tes não ten-ho me-nos nem

mais._ E os di-as pas-sem-ig-uais_

a-os di-as que vão dis-tan-tes. E os_ di-as pas-sem ig-

-uais_ a-os_ di-as que vão dis-tan-tes.

31

Ho-ras, min - u - tos e ins - tan - tes___ se - guem a or - dem aus -

- te - ra. Nin guém se a - gar - ra à quim - e - ra

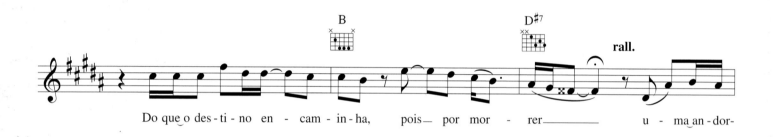

Do que o des - ti - no en - cam - in - ha, pois___ por mor - rer___ u - ma an - dor-

a tempo

- in - ha não a - ca - ba a Pri - ma - ve - ra. Por mor - rer___ u - ma an - dor - in -

- ha não_ a - ca - ba a Pri - ma - ve - ra.

1 Se deixaste de ser minha,
   Não deixei de ser quem era.
   Por morrer uma andorinha } *Repeat*
   Não acaba a Primavera.

2 Como vês não estou mudado,
   E nem sequer descontente,
   Conservo o mesmo presente } *Repeat*
   E guardo o mesmo passado.

3 Eu já estava habituado
   A que não fosses sincera,
   Por isso não fico à espera
   Duma ilusão que não tinha.
   Se deixaste de ser minha,
   Não deixei de ser quem era. } *Repeat*

4 Vivo a vida como dantes
   Não tenho menos nem mais.
   E os dias passem iguais
   Aos dias que vão distantes. } *Repeat*

5 Horas, minutos e instantes
   Seguem a ordem austera.
   Ninguém se agarra à quimera
   Do que o destino encaminha.
   Pois, por morrer uma andorinha } *Repeat*
   Não acaba a primavera.

Though I no longer call you mine
My life remains, and I am fine
Although a single swallow dies
The seasons change, the spring survives.

As you can see I have not changed
I still go on, I still maintain,
And now the present is the same,
Just as the past, it still remains.

And I knew well your lying ways,
So now I have no loss of faith,
And now the present is the same,
Just as the past, it still remains.

Just as before I count the days
The hours and minutes still parade
In perfect rhythm as they fade
No one can change the march of fate.

And even when the swallow's gone
The seasons change, the spring goes on.

Translation by Darryl Harris Cohen

O EMBUÇADO

The Masked Man

Gabriel d'Oliveira / Alcídia Rodrigues

'**O** EMBUÇADO represents an excellent illustration of how *fados* are sometimes borrowed and adapted. The song was co-written by Gabriel d'Oliveira, nicknamed 'Gabriel Marujo' (Gabriel the Sailor), a prominent poet in the first half of the last century, for the object of his affections, Maria Pereira, a well-known *fadista*.

The melody he borrowed had previously been entitled '*Fado Natalia*'. Others recorded '*O Embuçado*', which translates as 'the masked man', employing that same melody, including among them Manuel da Almeida, a marvellous singer of *fado* who performed well into the 1990s. Somewhere along the line another well-known performer, João Ferreira Rosa, added a verse and performed the lyrics to an older *fado* melody, and this version has become a classic. It is this second version which is represented in this collection.

'*O Embuçado*' is a good example of a *fado castiço*, (from the Latin term from which the English word 'caste' is derived). *Fado castiço*, (pronounced 'fadoo kast ee soo') can be rendered in English as 'true' or 'pure' *fado*. Among the typical subjects for this type of ballad are bullfighting, life and love during the time of the Portuguese kingdom, and the nobility itself. Bullfighting, as in Spain, is very popular in Portugal, although it is quite different in a number of ways. One of the most significant of these is that the bull is not killed in Portugal.

There are a significant number of *fados* about the nobility and the main reason for this can be found in the Portuguese attitude toward their noble families. Although the Portuguese abolished their kingdom in 1910, after the forced removal of their last King, Manuel II, and a revolution did, in fact, take place, there occurred no civil war or bloody confrontation leading to this event. Not only is there a clear lack of animosity toward the former nobility, many of whom continue to be leading members of society, but many Portuguese have a warm feeling towards the noble families, both past and present, considering them a valuable part of their historical tradition.

Although the particular event related in '*O Embuçado*' may be a fictional one, it is entirely possible that it, or a similar event, might have

occurred. Not only did *fado* become popular with the aristocracy, but also many wealthy and aristocratic families did indeed maintain 'salons' where they would entertain their noble, sometimes royal, guests and hire *fado* singers and musicians to perform. It was, and remains the custom for those who have the means, to hire *fadistas* to perform at holiday festivals and family celebrations.

From early times, in spite of *fado*'s initial questionable reputation, certain members of the nobility became well-respected writers and performers of *fado*. They continue that tradition to the present day. One of the greatest *fadistas* of this century, Maria Teresa de Noronha, was also the Condessa (Countess) de Sabrosa, while the present Duke de Braganza, of the royal house which once ruled Portugal, is sometimes heard in the *fado* houses singing *fado vadio*, a kind of impromptu performance for amateurs.

▼ One of the greatest *fadistas* of this century, Maria Teresa de Noronha

O EMBUÇADO

1. Nou - tro tem - po a fid - al - gui - a,
(Verses 2-4 see block lyrics)

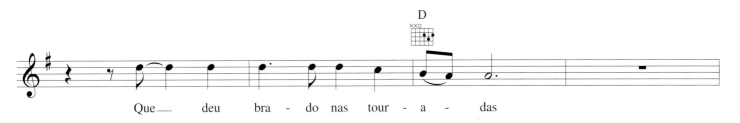

Que — deu bra - do nas tour - a - das

E an - da - va p'la — Mou - ra - ri - a, Em mui - to pal - ácio hav-

-i - a Des - cantes e guit - ar - ra - das.

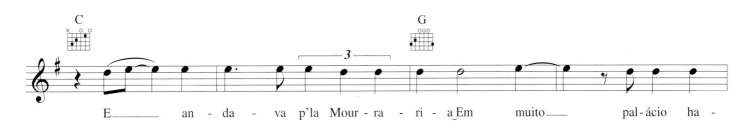

E — an - da - va p'la Mour - ra - ri - a Em muito — pal - ácio ha-

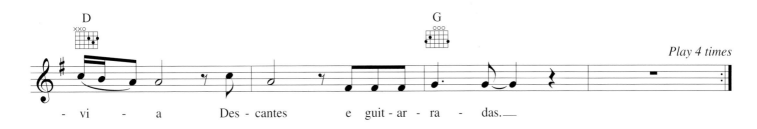

Play 4 times

-vi - a Des - cantes e guit - ar - ra - das.—

E p'rà ad - mir-a - çã - o ger - al_____

Des - co-bri-u - se o em-bu - ça - do,_____

Era_____ o Rei de_____ Port - u - gal,_____ hou - ve

bei - ja mão re - al E de - pois can - tou-se o fa - do.

Er - a_____ o Rei

de_____ Port - u - gal_____ hou - ve bei - ja mão re - al e dep-

- ois can - tou-se o fa - do.»

1   Noutro tempo a fidalguia,
       Que deu brado nas touradas
       E andava p'la Mouraria,
       Em muito palácio havia   } *Repeat*
       Descantes e guitarradas
	In the days of the nobility
	Who used to distinguish themselves at the bullfights
	And went to the Mouraria
	Where many palaces
	Presented ballad and guitar shows

2   E a história que eu vou contar,
       Contou uma certa velhinha
       «Uma vez que eu fui cantar,
       Ao salão dum titulado   } *Repeat*
       Lá pr'ò Paço da Rainha
	The story I am going to tell
	Was told to me by a certain old woman,
	"One time I went to sing
	At a nobleman's salon
	Near the Paço da Rainha

3   E nesse salão dourado,
       De ambiente nobre e sério
       Para ouvir cantar o fado,
       Ia sempre um embuçado   } *Repeat*
       Personagem de mistério
	In this golden salon
	Of noble and serious ambience
	There always appeared a masked man,
	A mysterious individual,
	Who came to listen to *fado*,

4   Mas certa noite houve alguém,
       Que lhe disse erguendo fala
       'Embuçado, nota bem,
       Que hoje não fique ninguém   } *Repeat*
       Embuçado nesta sala'
	But one night there was someone there
	Who firmly said these words to him:
	'Note well, masked man,
	Today there are no
	Masked men allowed in this hall'

5   E p'ra a admiração geral
       Descobriu-se o embuçado,
       Era o Rei de Portugal,
       Houve beija mão real   } *Repeat*
       E depois cantou-se o fado»
	To everyone's surprise
	The masked man removed his mask:
	It was the King of Portugal!
	The royal hand was kissed
	And afterwards *fado* was sung"

Bullfighting, as in Spain, is very popular in Portugal, although it is quite different in a number of ways. One of the most significant of these is that the bull is not killed in Portugal

A ROSINHA DOS LIMÕES

Little Rose Of The Lemons

Artur Joaquim de Alemeida Ribeiro

THIS VERY POPULAR *fado* takes as its subject matter one very often found in this musical form, particularly in the older *fados*, that of the street vendor. These were very popular individuals in Lisbon culture and songs about them were widespread. The vendors of lemons, oranges, flowers, etc., always female, were often idealised in *fados*, particularly in the earlier years (see *'Moda das Tranças Pretas'*, and *'Júlia Florista'* later). A particularly popular occupation with writers of *fado* was that of the 'varina', or female fish vendor, a figure that we will encounter several times in this collection.

These street vendors were frequently romanticised, often presented as sympathetic, sometimes tragic figures. One may recall that, in one of those instances where romance meets reality, the great Amália Rodrigues was discovered selling oranges along the Lisbon docks.

'A Rosinha dos Limões' has been likened in feeling to another great hit in the Portuguese language from the other side of the world, António Carlos Jobim and Vinicius de Moraes's 'The Girl From Ipanema', which utilises similar imagery about a similar subject.

The most popular recording of this song was made in March 1952 by a celebrated and widely recorded *fadista* who was known simply as 'Max'. His full name was Teodoro Silva Maximiliano de Sousa and, unlike most of the older singers of *fado,* he was not originally from Lisbon. Max was a native of the city of Funchal, capital of the Portuguese island of Madeira, on which the incomparable Madeira wines are produced. He early dreamed of becoming a barber and playing the violin, but he had little patience for the discipline for that instrument and ended his education by learning the tailor's craft.

Max first made his mark in 1936, singing in the small hotels of his native city, performing at night and tailoring by day before achieving recognition and going on to fame and fortune in Lisbon. In 1942 he co-founded a small band, serving as singer and drummer. After achieving great success on Madeira, the group went on to Lisbon in 1946. Achieving great acclaim in his performance of *fados*, he left the group in 1948 and began performing on Portuguese radio. At about the same time he signed a recording contract with Valentim de Carvalho, the prestigious musical recording company that continues to this day to represent many of *fado*'s finest artists.

Max also went on to achieve great success in the world of musical theatre, appearing in numerous shows and musical reviews. He toured widely, performing for Portuguese audiences in Angola, Mozambique, South Africa, Brazil, Argentina and the US.

He always continued, however, to sing the folk songs of his native island even as he was achieving his reputation as a *fadista*. A few of his Madeira island songs also became hits on the mainland of Portugal. Max was one of the most popular of the artists recording *fado* during the middle decades of the 20th Century, passing away in 1980.

▼ This acclaimed *fadista*, known only as 'Max' also popularised the songs of his native island, Madeira.

A ROSINHA DOS LIMÔES

♩=76

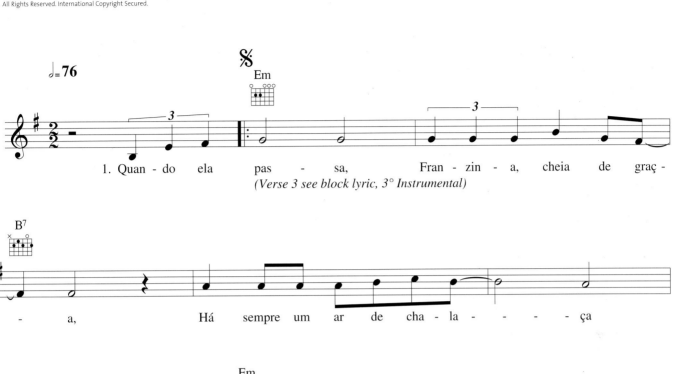

1. Quan - do ela pas - sa, Fran - zin - a, cheia de graç -

(Verse 3 see block lyric, 3° Instrumental)

- a, Há sempre um ar de cha - la - - - ça

No seu ol - har fei - ti - cei - ro. Lá vai cat - i - ta, ca - da

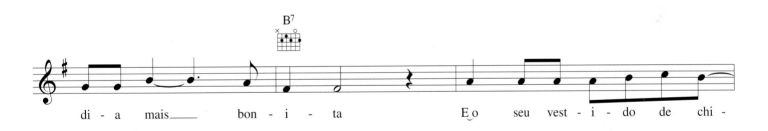

di - a mais bon - i - ta E o seu vest - i - do de chi -

To Coda ⊕

- ta tem sempre um ar dom - in - guei - ro. 2. Pas - sa li -

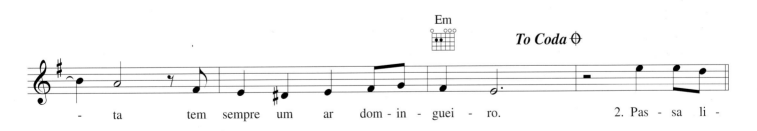

- gei - ra, A - le - gre e nam - or - a - dei - ra

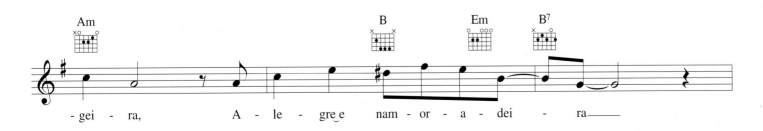

E a sor - rir p'rá rua in - tei - ra, Vai sem - e - an - do il - usões.

Quan - do ela pas - - sa, Vai

ven - der lim - ões à pra - ça e at - é lhe cha - mam, por gra -

- ça,——— «A Ros -in - ha dos Lim - ões.» 3. Quan - do ela pas -

2° D.%. al Coda

⊕ Coda

4. Quan - - do ela pas - sa A - pre - go - an - do os

lim - ões——— A sós, «com os meus bot - õ - es.»——— No

vão da min - ha jan - e - - la Fi - co pen -

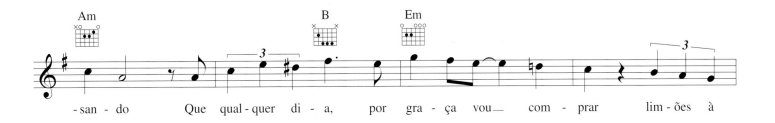

-san - do   Que qual - quer di - a,   por gra - ça vou___ com - prar   lim - ões à

rit.

pra - ça   E de - pois___ caso com e - la!

1 Quando ela passa,
   Franzina, cheia de graça,
   Há sempre um ar de chalaça
   No seu olhar feiticeiro.
   Lá vai catita,
   Cada dia mais bonita
   E o seu vestido de chita
   Tem sempre um ar domingueiro.

2 Passa ligeira,
   Alegre e namoradeira
   E a sorrir p'rá rua inteira,
   Vai semeando ilusões.
   Quando ela passa,
   Vai vender limões à praça
   E até lhe chamam, por graça,
   «A Rosinha dos Limões».

3 Quando ela passa
   Junto á minha janela,
   Meus olhos vão atrás dela,
   Até ver da rua o fim.
   Com ar gaiato,
   Ela caminha apressada,
   Rindo por tudo e por nada
   E, às vezes, sorri p'ra mim!

4 Quando ela passa
   Apregoando os limões
   A sós, «com os meus botões»
   No vão da minha janela
   Fico pensando
   Que qualquer dia, por graça,
   Vou comprar limões à praça
   E depois caso com ela!

When she passes by
Slender and full of grace,
Always with a mocking air
In her bewitching look.
She moves elegantly
Prettier every day,
And her chintz dress
Always has a Sunday look.

Lightly she passes
Cheerful and coquettish,
And, smiling to everyone,
She spreads illusions.
When she passes, she's on her way
To sell lemons at the market
So they call her, jokingly,
"Little Rose of the Lemons".

When she passes by
Near my window,
My eyes follow her
'Til the end of the street.
With a mischievous air
She moves swiftly,
Laughing at everything and nothing
And, at times, she even smiles at me!

When she passes
Crying out, 'Lemons!',
Alone, I start to ponder.
While leaning on the window-sill,
I sit wondering
If, one day, I just might
Go to the market to buy lemons
And marry her!

When she passes by
Near my window,
My eyes follow her
'Til the end of the street.
With a mischievous air
She moves swiftly,
Laughing at everything
and nothing
And, at times, she even
smiles at me!

VINTE ANOS

Twenty Years

Frederico Valério / Nelson de Barros

'**V**INTE ANOS', ('twenty years') was also recorded under the title '*O Meu Primeiro Amor*' (My First Love). The distribution of recordings of the same song under two different titles is unusual but does happen in the world of *fado*, particularly with some of the older songs. As mentioned previously, borrowing and adapting of both lyrics and music was very common with traditional *fado* and persists, in fact, to this day.

This song was composed by two leading writers of *fado* – Frederico Valério and Nelson de Barros. Frederico Valério held a particularly prominent position in the world of *fado*. He was a poet, and one of the most prolific contemporary composers of incomparable *fado*s. Valério was born in Lisbon in 1913. He became an accomplished musician at an early age and began composing when he was 13. In the early 1940s he met Amália Rodrigues and it was with his songs that she had some of her greatest successes.

Of particular interest is the fact that in the late Forties Valério decided to fulfil his dream of travelling to America. He not only accomplished this but also succeeded in breaking into the music scene in New York where he wrote a number of recorded melodies in English. One of his songs, 'Don't Say Goodbye', was a juke-box hit.

Valério was equally at home in France where his song '*Les Cloches de Lisbonne*' was extremely popular. He always claimed that all of his melodies had a Portuguese foundation and he firmly believed that had he not maintained this integrity, had he been merely imitative of American or French musical trends, his efforts would have been immediately rejected. Valério died in 1982.

Nelson de Barros, one of Portugal's finest composers of *fado*, often collaborated with Amália Rodrigues, and frequently wrote new material for her.

'*Vinte Anos*' although recorded a number of times under both previously mentioned titles, was recorded with particular success by Celeste Rodrigues, the very talented and extremely popular sister of Amália. She considers it a particularly beautiful song; one of her favourites. This editor has, on several occasions, heard her humming or singing snatches of it to herself. A woman of great charm but also of strong opinions, particularly with regard to *fado,* Senhora Rodrigues took a dislike to several lines of lyric and whenever she performs this song she has the orchestra fill in those lines as an instrumental.

Celeste Rodrigues (pictured right) was born in Fundão, near the Estrela Mountains in central Portugal in 1922. She came to Lisbon when she was five years old. Celeste began singing in the typical Lisbon *fado* restaurants in 1945. Her recordings reflect a full, rich, sensuous voice and a compelling vocal style. Popular in Portugal, she performs frequently on Portuguese radio and television as well as in England, Belgium, Spain, Africa, Brazil and the United States.

◄ The hands of a *fadista* expressing *saudade*.

How I wish I could be
disillusioned once again
How I wish I was twenty again,
to love you again

VINTE ANOS

♩ = 100

Dm   A   Dm   D⁹/F♯   Gm

1. Ai,   quem me de — ra   ter ou - tra vez   vinte a - nos.
(3° Instrumental)

C   C⁷   F

Ai,   como eu era___   como te amei,   San - to Deus.

A⁷   Dm   A⁷

Meus láb - ios   pare - ci-am   dois franc - iscan-os___

Gm   A⁷   Dm

Á es - pe — ra   do sol___   que vinha dos teus.___

A⁷   Dm   D⁷   Gm

2. Bei — jos que eu da - va,   ai,   como quem morde ro - sas
(Verse 4 see block lyric)

C   F

Como   te espera - - - va   vi - da que então___   vi - vi.

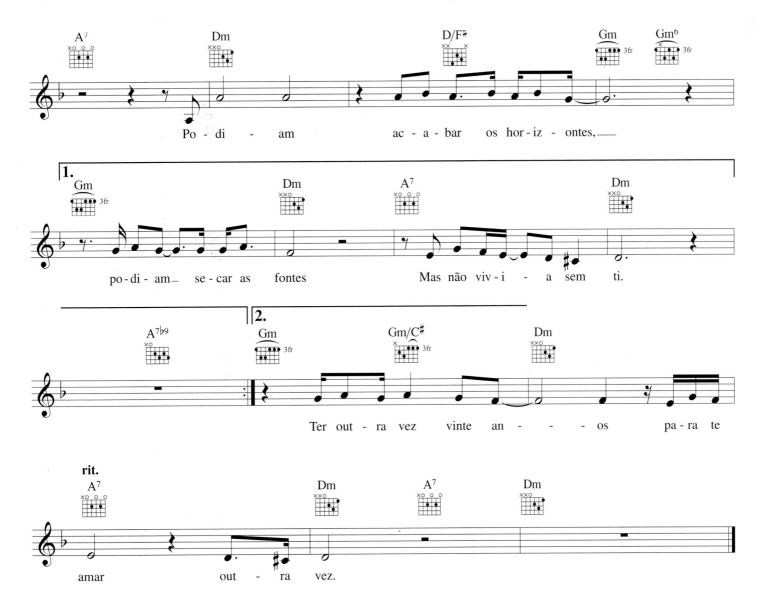

1 Ai, quem me dera ter outra vez vinte anos.
  Ai, como eu era, como te amei, Santo Deus.
  Meus lábios pareciam dois franciscanos
  À espera do sol que vinha dos teus.

  Oh, how I wish I was twenty again,
  Oh, how I was, how I loved, Holy God.
  My lips waiting for yours
  Were like two Franciscans waiting for the sun.

2 Beijos que eu dava, ai, como quem morde rosas
  Como te esperava vida que então vivi.
  Podiam acabar os horizontes, podiam secar as fontes
  Mas não vivia sem ti.

  The kisses that I used to give, it was like biting roses.
  How I waited for you, the life I then lived.
  The horizons could end, the fountains run dry
  But I couldn't live without you..

3 Ai, como é triste de o dizer, não me envergonho,
  Saber que existe um ser tão mau e ruim.
  Tu que eras o sonho para o meu sonho
  Traíste o melhor que havia em mim.

  Oh, how sad it is to say it, I'm not ashamed
  To know that there is a being so evil.
  You that were the dream of my dream
  You betrayed the best that was in me.

4 Ai, como o tempo pôs neve nos teus cabelos.
  Ai, como o tempo as nossas vidas desfez.
  Quem dera ter outra vez desenganos,
  Ter outra vez vinte anos para te amar outra vez.

  Oh, how time has put snow on your hair,
  Oh, how time has undone our lives.
  How I wish I could be disillusioned once again.
  How I wish I was twenty again, to love you again.

E FOI-SE A MOCIDADE

And Youth Is Gone

João Nobre Dias / Domingos Gonçalves Costa

'E FOI-SE A MOCIDADE' (And Youth Is Gone) is one of many popular *fados* made famous by a beloved singer of the mid-20th Century, Carlos Ramos. This is neither a traditional nor a classic *fado*, but one of the more modern ballads often described as '*fado musicado*' or '*fado canção*', to distinguish them from the more traditional forms.

Ramos was born in 1907, in the ancient Alcântara district of Lisbon, an area steeped in *fado*. Here he was engulfed in the music from his early years. After studying radio communications and spending some time as a specialist in the Army, Ramos resigned in order to devote himself entirely to *fado* in 1944.

He began his career as an accomplished performer and accompanist on the Portuguese guitar, and his career as a singer was the result of mere chance. It was a question of being in the right place at the right time. One evening at an important performance, the scheduled singer failed to appear and Ramos was induced to fill in. And fill in he did. So well, in fact, that soon Ramos's became one of the most important *fado* voices of his era and remained so until his death in 1969.

This remarkable performer's voice was not large or trained. It is conjectural whether he would have found success as a singer of popular music in other musical venues or in other countries. But his voice possessed a quality of warmth and depth of feeling that made him a most compelling interpreter of the *fado* genre.

Ramos rarely sang traditional *fado*. He was, it appears, not as comfortable in a form which required extemporaneous expression. He preferred performing the newer songs being written during that very prolific period of enduring *fado* creations.

His first album, entitled *O Melhor de Carlos Ramos* (The Best Of Carlos Ramos), was an immediate smash hit, and he gained an immense and loyal following. Other recordings soon followed. So moving were his interpretations of these *fados* that, not only did a number of these songs become immortal, but also they have remained totally identified with him to this day.

This particular selection is also memorable for another reason. The guitar accompaniment for this particular song is one of the most beautifully rendered of any in this collection and, in fact, that we have ever heard. It was the work of one of the best and most important Portuguese guitarists in the history of the art form known simply and affectionately as '*Carvalinho*' and with him on the viola, i.e. the Spanish guitar, was Martin d'Assuncão, another of most notable figures in his field. The *conjunto* (instrumental group) of Martin d'Assuncão was one of the two most famous accompaniment groups in the *fado* world, the other being the *conjunto* of Raul Nery which is discussed later in this book.

The word '*boémia*' (bohemian), in the third verse of this song, is one frequently to be found, along with the word '*bizarro*' (bizarre) in *fados* where descriptions of the people and times of the early *fado* are being rendered. This is because of the association of the *fadista* with the arty, unconventional, nonconformist element of Lisbon society; an association alluded to not only by other elements of Portuguese society, but, proudly, by the *fadistas* themselves.

◀ The exceptional singer Carlos Ramos was also a talented Portuguese guitarist.

E FOI-SE A MOCIDADE

♩=80

1. Sin - to sau - da - - de quan - do passo àquel - a
(Verse 2 see block lyric)

rua on - de min - ha moc - i - da - - de par - e -

-ce que ainda flu - tua,___ Sau - dade e - nor - me de re -

-ver ne - sses por - tais___ A minha in - fân - cia que dorm - e se -

___ des - per - tar___ nun - ca mais. E à noite a sós julgo ou -

-vir cheio de es - peran - - ça A min - ha voz___ cris - ta -

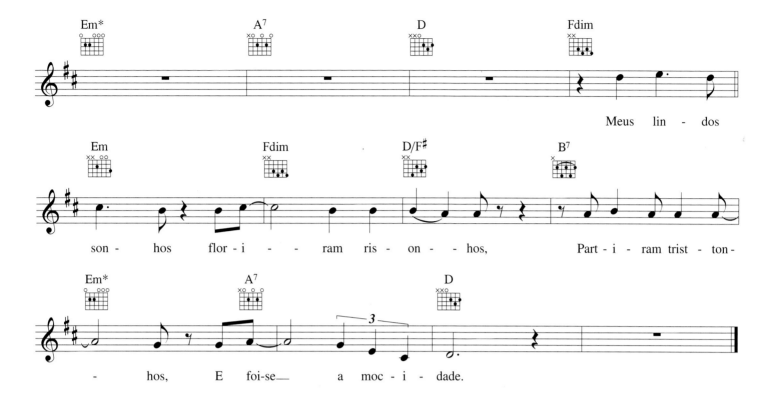

Meus lin - dos son - hos flor - i - - ram ris - on - - hos, Part - i - ram trist - ton- - hos, E foi-se— a moc - i - dade.

1	Sinto saudade quando passo àquela rua	I feel *saudade* when I pass that street
	Onde a minha mocidade parece que ainda flutua,	Where my youth appears to be floating still,
	Saudade enorme de rever nesses portais	Enormous *saudade* to view again those portals
	A minha infância que dorme	Where my childhood sleeps,
	Sem despertar nunca mais.	never to wake again.
	E à noite a sós julgo ouvir cheio de esperança	And alone at night I think I hear, full of hope,
	A minha voz cristalina de criança,	My voice as a child, crystal clear.
2	Mas hoje a vida, é estrada comprida,	But today life is a long road,
	Escarpada subida, à luz da realidade	a steep inclined hill in the light of reality
	Meus lindos sonhos floriram risonhos,	My lovely dreams that smilingly flourished
	Partiram tristonhos,	have sadly departed
	E foi-se a mocidade.	And youth is gone
3	Quemdera agora cantar formosas cantigas	I wish I could now sing beautiful songs
	Que eu cante pela noite fora	That I sang all night long
	Por essas ruas antigas,	in these old streets,
	Acompanhado da boémia que passou,	Accompanied by the revellers that passed by
	Homens amigos do fado	Old friends of the *fado*,
	Que a morte há muito levou,	that death has taken long ago.
	Homens antigos por quem a guitarra chora	Old men for whom the guitar weeps,
	Velhos amigos quem dera vê-los agora.	Old friends that I wish I could see once again.
4	Hoje os meus fados são mais contristados,	Today my *fado*s are more saddened, pained,
	São ais magoados, murmúrios de saudade,	Whispers of *saudade*
	E estas cantigas, lembranças antigas	And those songs, old remembrances,
	São esperanças amigas,	are friendly hopes
	Da minha mocidade.	Of my youth.
	Meus lindos sonhos floriram risonhos,	My lovely dreams that smilingly flourished
	Partiram tristonhos,	have sadly departed
	E foi-se a mocidade.	And youth is gone

MEU BAIRRO ALTO

My Bairro Alto

Joaquim Frederico de Brito / José Carlos Rocha

THIS *FADO*, with lyrics by one of Portugal's finest writers of *fado*, Frederico de Brito, has been a popular hit for many years and has been recorded by a number of the most popular *fadistas* such as Carlos Ramos, Tristão da Silva, and, among the more contemporary performers, Nuno da Câmara Pereira.

It is a classic *fado* in that its subject is the ancient Bairro Alto district itself, one of the oldest areas of the city and one of those that gave birth to *fado*. It is in this hilltop neighbourhood (the words '*Bairro Alto*' translate as the 'high district') with its narrow winding streets and alleys, that a great many of the oldest and best *fado* houses are found.

Every night the Bairro Alto is filled with tourists and locals in cars, taxis and on foot, heading for the *fado* clubs, restaurants, and discos. Some of the former are large, commercial affairs with a large staff and a number of singers and musicians. Others have as few as a half dozen tables; a waitress, cook or even doorman doubling as the singer, with the owner and the dishwasher accompanying on Portuguese guitar and viola.

Colourful little yellow trolleys wind along the thoroughfare bordering this ancient district, and these, together with the antiquated, picturesque buildings, often decorated in tiles two or three centuries old, evoke in one a feeling that they have stepped back in time to the Portugal of the Empire.

The particular version of this *fado* presented here is performed by Nuno da Câmara Pereira. Born in 1951, he is a younger member of one of the most illustrious traditional *fado* families. He is related to two prominent *fadistas* – Maria Teresa de Noronha and Don Vicente da Câmara. Nuno da Câmara Pereira, however, from his first public appearance in

1977, quickly rose to prominence as one of the most promising talents of the Lisbon *fado* scene. His great success can be attributed to his pleasing style and artful delivery, coupled with a unique vocal quality that make his performances memorable.

After achieving success in live performances in both *fado* clubs and on the concert circuit, Periera recorded his first disc in 1982, which was an immediate success and a number of recordings rapidly followed. Shortly thereafter, and continuing throughout the Eighties and Nineties, Pereira toured much of Europe, Brazil, Africa, Canada and the United States.

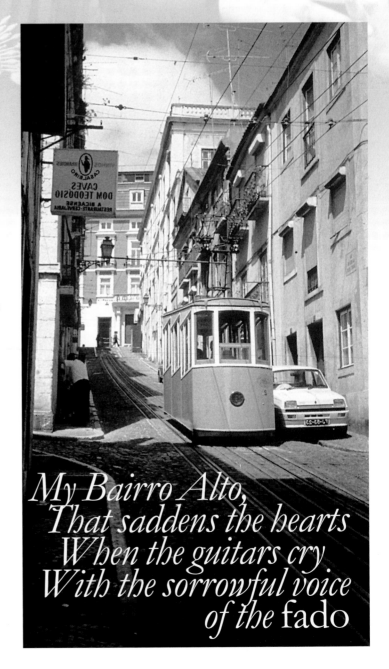

*My Bairro Alto,
That saddens the hearts
When the guitars cry
With the sorrowful voice
of the* fado

◀ Nuno da Câmara Pereira

54

MEU BAIRRO ALTO

♩=90

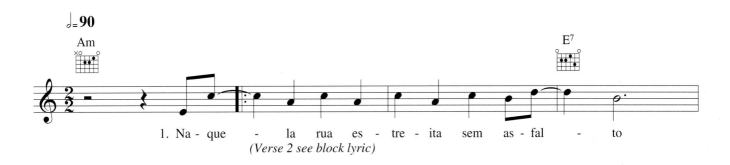

1. Na - que - la rua es - tre - ita sem as - fal - to
(Verse 2 see block lyric)

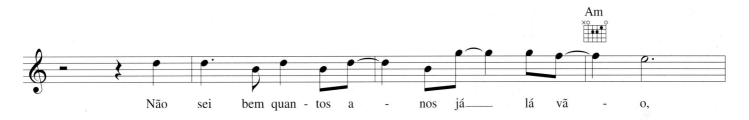

Não sei bem quan - tos a - nos já___ lá vã - o,

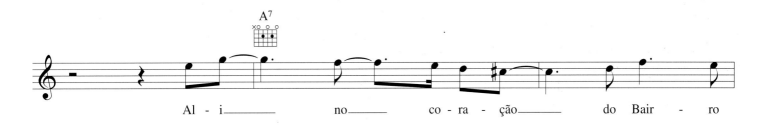

Al - i_____ no____ co - ra - ção____ do Bair - ro

Al - to,_____ Al - guém fez____ de ma - deira____

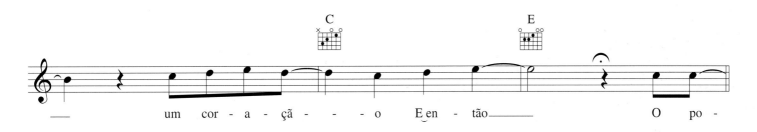

___ um cor - a - çã - - o E en - tão____ O po -

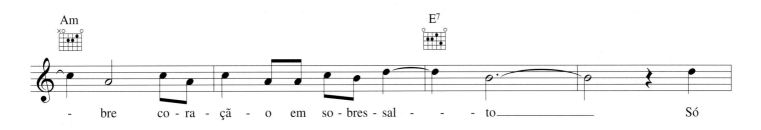

- bre co - ra - çã - o em so - bres - sal - - to_____ Só

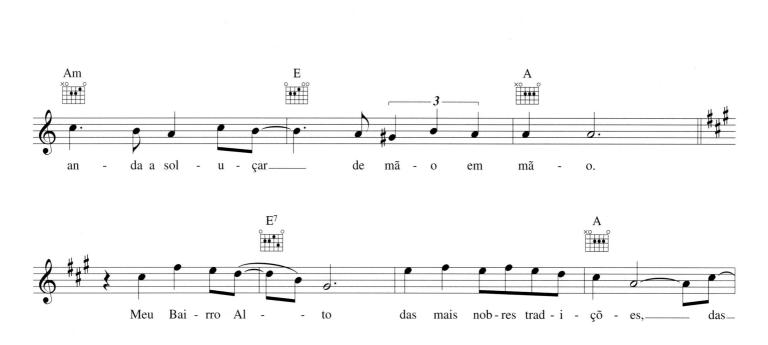

an - da a sol - u - çar____ de mã - o em mã - o.

Meu Bai - rro Al - to das mais nob - res trad - i - çõ - es,____ das____

____ fad - is - tas mais bi - zar - ras,____ dos bo - ém - ios do pas - sa - do.

Meu Bair - ro Al - to, que en - tris - tece____ os cor - a - çõ - es

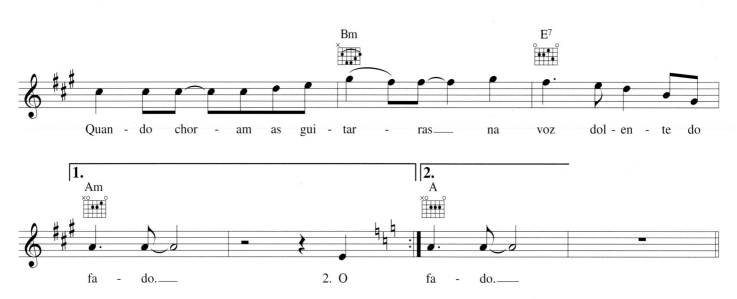

Quan - do chor - am as gui - tar - ras____ na voz dol - en - te do

| **1.** | **2.** |

fa - do.____   2. O   fa - do.____

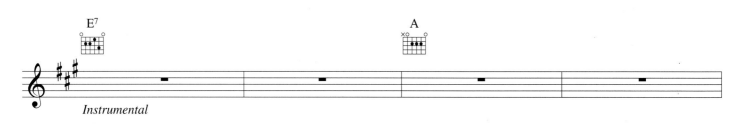

Instrumental

Meu Bai - rro Al - to que en - tris - tece os cor a -

- çõ - es quan - do chor - am as guit - ar - ras na

voz dol - en - te do fa - do.

1   Naquela rua estreita sem asfalto
    Não sei bem quantos anos já lá vão,
    Ali no coração do Bairro Alto,
    Alguém fez de madeira um coração e então
    O pobre coração em sobressalto
    Só anda a soluçar de mão em mão.

    Refrain
    Meu Bairro Alto,
    Das mais nobres tradições,
    Das fadistas mais bizarras,
    Dos boémios do passado.

    Meu Bairro Alto,
    Que entristece os corações
    Quando choram as guitarras
    Na voz dolente do fado.

2   O fado que é cantado e é «falado»
    Que tem uma guitarra para chorar,
    Que traz na voz um choro tão magoado
    A voz duma guitarra saudade a soluçar
    Ao ar
    O fado é sempre o mesmo
    É sempre o fado
    Que põe as almas tristes a sonhar

    Refrain

On that narrow unpaved street
I don't recall how many years have passed
There in the heart of Bairro Alto
Someone made a heart of wood,
And now the poor, trembling heart
Goes from hand to hand, sobbing:

Refrain
My Bairro Alto
Of the noblest traditions,
Of the colourful *fadistas*
Of the bohemians of the past.

My Bairro Alto,
That saddens the hearts
When the guitars cry
With the sorrowful voice of the *fado*.

The *fado* that is sung with feeling and expression,
That has a guitar to weep,
That brings to the voice a cry so pained.
And in the air,
The voice of a sobbing guitar.
Fado is always the same
It's always *fado*
That sets sad souls to dreaming

VALEU A PENA

It Was Worth It

Moniz Pereira

I CONFESS THAT this particular *fado* has had a special hold upon me ever since I first heard it, over three decades ago. Its quiet whimsy, suffused with an overwhelming poignancy, has made it impossible for me to listen to it without being profoundly moved.

The most evocative interpretation of this song was that rendered by the great Carlos Ramos whose voice, while not big, seems to sweep over you in a wave of feeling. This very popular performer made many hit recordings from the 1940s to the middle of the 1960s. Never a great interpreter of traditional *fado*, which requires the gift of being able to extemporise in performance, Ramos was at his best in selecting particularly haunting and evocative melodies and interpreting them so movingly that many of them have become ageless classics. Ramos's accompanist and music arranger was usually Raul Nery, a very important figure in *fado* for many decades. Nery was,

at one time or another, the guitarist and arranger for many prominent *fadistas*, including Amália and Carlos do Carmo.

In recording '*Valeu a Pena*', Carlos Ramos, for some reason, sang only the first verse of the song. He may have done this with a sense that the deep feeling it evoked would be more moving and profound with brevity. Other singers have included the second verse when performing '*Valeu a Pena*'. One of the most popular of the later interpreters is the gifted performer Maria da Fé, the celebrated proprietress of '*Senhor Vinho*', a very popular Lisbon *fado* venue. Da Fé's approach to this song is more forceful and passionate, in contrast to Ramos's gentle, wistful style.

▼ An outdoor *fado* performance in the Alfama, the most ancient district of Lisbon. Outdoor concerts were quite common in good weather, sometimes planned, but often impromptu. This was often the only way the inhabitants of these poorer districts could hear live performances.

VALEU A PENA

1. Com voz___ se - re - na pre - gun - tar - am - me ao ou-

-vi - do, val - eu a pena___

vir ao mun-do, ter nas - ci - do? Com leal -

-da - de vou res - pon - der Mas pri - meir - o con - sul -

-te - i meu trav-ess - eiro sobre___ a ver-dade___

Tive___ por - é - m de lem - brar - me de todo___ a pass-a-

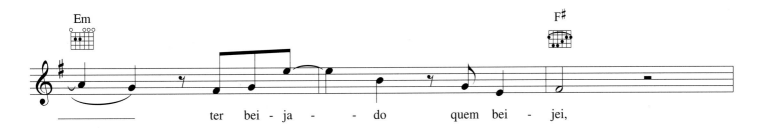

ter bei - ja - - do quem bei - jei,

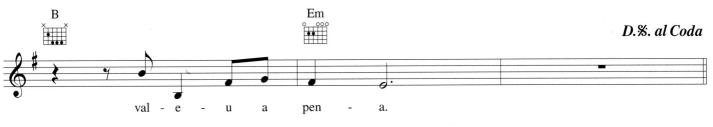

D.%. al Coda

val - e - u a pen - a.

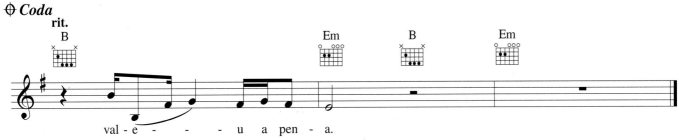

val - e - - u a pen - a.

1 Com voz serena perguntaram-me ao ouvido,
Valeu a pena vir ao mundo, ter nascido?
Com lealdade vou responder
Mas primeiro consultei
Meu travesseiro sobre a verdade,
Tive porém de lembrar-me de todo a passado,
Horas boas do meu fado
E as más também.

Refrain
Valeu a pena ter vivido o que vivi,
Valeu a pena ter sofrido o que sofri,
Valeu a pena ter amado quem amei,
Ter beijado quem beijei, valeu a pena .

2 Valeu a pena ter sonhado o que sonhei,
Valeu a pena ter passado o que passei,
Valeu a pena ter conhecido o que conheci,
Ter sentido o que senti,
Valeu a pena,
Valeu a pena ter cantado o que cantei,
Ter chorado o que chorei,
Valeu a pena.

Refrain

With a quiet voice
They ask me, whispering,
"Was it worth it?
To come into the world, to have been born?"
Faithfully I wanted to answer,
But first I consulted my pillow
For the truth.
I had, however, to remember all of the past,
The good hours spent with the *fado*,
And the bad ones as well.

Refrain
It was worth living as I have lived
It was worth suffering what I suffered
It was worth loving who I loved
Kissing whom I kissed,
It was worth it.

It was worth it to have dreamed what I dreamed
It was worth it to have experienced what I experienced
It was worth it to have known what I knew
To have felt what I felt,
It was worth it.
It was worth it to have sung what I sung
To have cried as I have cried,
It was worth it.

Refrain

ROSA ENJEITADA

Abandoned Rose

José Galhardo / Raul Ferrão

THIS BEAUTIFUL SONG is the result of another glorious collaboration between those two master creators of the *fado* art form, José Galhardo and Raul Ferrão. The subject matter is a typical one in Lisbon *fado*, the fallen and/or abandoned woman, betrayed by love and life. For other examples in this collection alone, the reader has only to refer to '*Ai, Mouraria*', '*Fado da Defesa*', and '*Maria Madalena*'. '*Rosa Enjeitada*' has been the subject of recordings by many singers, including recently the *fadista* Margarida Bessa, but is first and foremost associated in the eyes of the public with Maria Teresa de Noronha.

The fact is that the title and perhaps the identical subject of the *fado* itself had achieved prominence in Portugal at an earlier period, but in a different form. '*Rosa Enjeitada*' is the title of a play written in 1901 by Don João Gonçalves Zarco da Câmara, one of the most prominent dramatists of the Portuguese theatre at the end of the 19th Century and the beginning of the 20th. One Portuguese literary critic wrote, in 1903, that '*Rosa Enjeitada*', which can be translated as 'abandoned rose' or 'rejected rose', was one of the most beautiful dramas that he had seen in his life.

It has been mentioned previously that *fado* is a genre in which the higher, middle and lower classes of Portuguese society interacted and to which representatives of all three classes contributed. The singer Maria Teresa de Noronha is one of the best examples of the contribution of the aristocracy to the *fado* phenomenon.

Born Maria Teresa do Carmo de Noronha, in Lisbon, in 1918 to a prominent noble family, it early became apparent that she was possessed of a crystal clear, compelling voice, and a distinctive style. Soon after she began singing, Noronha was invited to initiate a weekly programme for a new radio station, and she continued to perform in that radio spot every week for 23 consecutive years until her retirement.

This excellent performer was also related to the great da Camara family of *fadistas* in that she was the aunt of Don Vicente da Câmara, the senior member of that performing clan, and thus was related to the playwright D. João Zarco da Câmara mentioned above. Noronha became Countess of Sabrosa by marriage in 1947. Her forte was the classic *fado* and *fado castiço* and it is on her interpretation of these particular forms that her incomparable reputation rests.

It seems appropriate, at this point, to discuss another very important figure in the world of *fado* associated with Maria Teresa de Noronha – Raul Nery. However, Nery could also be discussed in association with any number of the finest *fadistas* because he worked closely with many of them and contributed greatly to the success of their performances and recordings.

Born in Lisbon in 1921, Raul Nery was not only one of the greatest exponents of the Portuguese guitar in the second half of the last century, but he founded one of the most influential *fado* guitar groups of that era. Already playing for private parties at the age of nine, Nery was, at 16, an accompanist for the great *fadista* Ercilia Costa, nicknamed the *Santa do Fado* (Saint of the *fado*), and a year later was a part of the instrumental group playing at the celebrated club '*Retiro da Severa*'.

During the length of his extensive career, Nery was selected to accompany some of the biggest names in the field, such as Herminia Silva, Berta Cardoso, Amália, Carlos do Carmo and finally, Maria Teresa de Noronha, whose exclusive guitarist he was for 20 years. In 1959 Nery formed the *Conjunto de Guitarras de Raul Nery*, together with Júlio Gomes, Joel Pina, and José Fontes Rocha. Rocha is considered by many to be the finest *fado* guitarist playing today. This group continued in existence for 10 years accompanying the top singers on records and in television programmes throughout Portugal. Raul Nery retired in 1980.

ROSA ENJEITADA

♩=68

Free time

1. Sou es - sa

A tempo

Ro - sa, ca - pri - cho - sa, sem— ser má .
(Verse 2 see block lyric)

Flor d'al - ma pu - ra, e de ter - nu - ra, ao Deus da - rá. —

Que viu um di - a, que sen -

-ti - a um - gran - de a - mor.— E de paix - ão, —

—— o - co - ra - çao e - - sta - lar de dor.

63

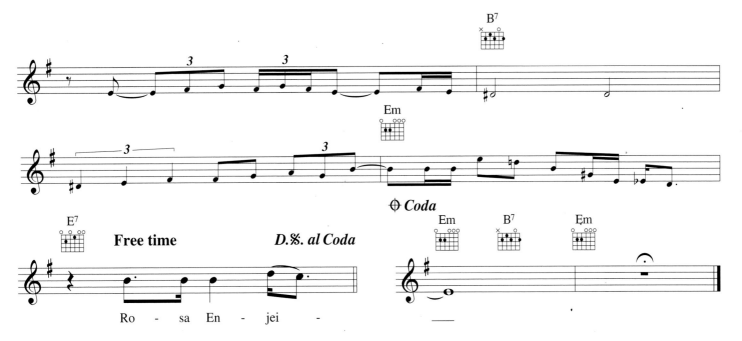

Free time

D.%. al Coda

⊕ *Coda*

Ro - sa En - jei -

1 Sou essa Rosa
   Caprichosa
   Sem ser má
   Flor d'alma pura
   E de ternura
   Ao Deus dará
   Que viu um dia
   Que sentia
   Um grande amor
   E de paixão
   O coraçao
   Estalar de dor

   Refrain
   Rosa Enjeitada
   Sem mãe, sem pãe, sem ter nada
   Que vida triste e chorada
   O teu destino te deu
   Rosa Enjeitada
   Rosa humilde e perfumada
   E afinal desventurada quem és tu
   Rosa Enjeitada
   Uma mulher que sofreu

2 Tão pobrezhinha
   Ainda tinha uma ilusão
   Alguém que amava
   Em quem sonhava
   Uma afeição
   Mas esse alguém
   Por outro bem
   Se apaixonou
   E assim fiquei
   Sem ele que amei
   Que me enjeitou

   Refrain

I am that Rose,
Capricious
But not wicked,
The flower of a pure soul
Tender, as God wills,
Who one day realised that
She felt a great love,
And from passion
Her heart burst with pain.

Refrain
Abandoned Rose
Without a mother, without a father, without anything
What a sad, tearful life
Fate gave you
Abandoned rose,
Humble, perfumed Rose
And finally, in the end, unlucky
Who are you,
Abandoned Rose,
A woman who suffered

So destitute and alone,
She still had an illusion
Someone she loved
Of whom she dreamt,
A passion,
But that someone
Fell in love with another
And so I was left
Without the one I loved
Who abandoned me

Abandoned Rose
Without a mother, without
a father, without anything
What a sad, tearful life
Fate gave you
Abandoned rose,
Humble, perfumed Rose
And finally, in the end,
unlucky
Who are you,
Abandoned Rose,
A woman who suffered

FADO HILÁRIO

Augusto Hilário da Costa Alves

THIS IS A perfect example of a traditional Coimbra *fado* and one of the most famous of that genre. The composer, Augusto Hilário da Costa Alves – known to all lovers of Coimbra *fado* simply as 'Hilário' – was born in the ancient city of Viseu. There is considerable dispute as to the year of his birth; possibly 1864 but more likely 1872, as his age at death in 1904 is usually recorded as 32. He entered the University of Coimbra to begin studies as a physician, but quickly achieved great fame as a songwriter and singer of Coimbra *fado*. The call of the music and the bohemian life of the student so enraptured him that he never went beyond the third year of medicine.

There are few photographs of Hilário and very little information concerning his life. There have been persistent rumours of a recording session sometime in the years preceding his death and even of the possible survival of an early recording cylinder, but none has ever been found.

▼ Augusto Hilário da Costa Alves, universally know simply as 'Hilário', is credited with redefining and popularising the Coimbra *fado*.

A number of *fados* were composed and continue to be sung in his honour and these attribute to him the introduction of Lisbon *fado* to the University of Coimbra and its adaptation to Coimbra musical traditions. How much of this is fact and how much myth is unclear. As stated in the Introduction, there existed a rich musical tradition based upon Provençal and, to some extent, Moorish and Sephardic (Jewish) medieval stylised ballad forms. But what is undeniable is that, during his short life, Hilário, probably together with his disciples, redefined and popularised the Coimbra style of *fado* for succeeding generations of students and faculty, both singers and guitarists.

As early as 1906 the singer Avelino Baptista had recorded a version of *'Fado Hilário'*, and Eugénio Noronha recorded it again in 1911. The great Maria Teresa de Noronha also had great success performing this particular song in the middle decades of the last century.

Sometime in the late 1940s or early 1950s the melody of *'Fado Hilário'* was included in the Portuguese film *Capas Negras*, with new lyrics honouring its famous creator sung by the star of the film, Alberto Ribeiro. The title *'Capas Negras'* (black capes) refers to the capes traditionally worn by the students at the University of Coimbra, the wearing of which also became traditional when singing Coimbra *fado*.

The lyrics included in this collection are the original ones penned by Hilário himself. This version of the song is one recorded by a very prominent, gifted singer of Coimbra *fado*, a lawyer and graduate of the University of Coimbra, Luís Goes. The third verse, while it may be one of Hilário's original verses, is not included in the Goes recording.

The term *'dum vencido'* in the second verse is rendered in the English translation as 'of a 'vanquished'', using the word 'vanquished' as a noun. It refers to a literary circle called *'Os Vencidos da Vida'* (The Defeated In Life). This group, which existed in Portugal in the latter part of the 19th Century, included many of the nation's finest writers and poets among its members.

FADO HILÁRIO

A min - ha ca - pa ve - lhi - nha, é da cor da noite es -

- cu - ra. A min - ha ca - pa ve - lhi - nha, é da cor da noite es -

- cu - ra. Ne - la que - ro a - mort-al - har - me. Quan -

do for p'rà se - pul - tu - ra! Ne - la que - ro a - mort-al - har - me. Ai, quan -

do for p'rà se - pul - tu - ra! Ela há - de cont - ar aos ver - - mes Ai, ja

que eu não pos - so fa - lar, Ela há - de cont - ar aos ver - - mes Ai, ja

que eu não pos - so fa - lar,____ Se - gre - dos ru - bor - i -

- za - dos ai da minha al - m'a sol - u - çar.____ Eu

que - ro que o meu cai - xão,____ ten - ha u - ma for - ma bi -

- zar - ra:____ Eu__ que - ro que o meu cai - xão,____ ten -

- ha u - ma for - ma bi - zar - ra:____ A__ for - ma de dum cor - a -

- ção,____ ai a for - ma du - ma gui - tar - ra! A

for - ma de dum cor - a - ção,____ ai a for - ma du - ma qui - tar - ra!

1	A minha capa velhinha É da cor da noite escura.	*Repeat*	My gown that is now so old, Is the colour of a dark night.	*Repeat*

1   A minha capa velhinha / É da cor da noite escura.   *Repeat*   My gown that is now so old, / Is the colour of a dark night.   *Repeat*

   Nela quero amortalhar-me, / Quando for p'rà sepultura !   *Repeat*   I want it to serve as my shroud, / When I go to my grave!   *Repeat*

2   Ela há-de contar aos vermes, / Ai, ja que eu não posso falar,   *Repeat*   It will tell the worms, / Since I can no longer speak,   *Repeat*

   Segredos ruborizados / Ai, da minha alm'a soluçar.   Blushing secrets / Out of my sobbing soul.   *Repeat*

3   A minha capa ondulante / Feita de negro tecido,   *Repeat*   My gown that furls around me / Made of the blackest stuff,   *Repeat*

   Não é capa de estudante: / É mortalha dum vencido!   *Repeat*   Is not the gown of a student, / It is the shroud of a 'vanquished'!   *Repeat*

4   Ai… Eu quero que o meu caixão / Tenha uma forma bizarra: *Repeat*   I want my coffin to have / An exotic design.   *Repeat*

   A forma de dum coração / Ai… A forma duma guitarra!   *Repeat*   The form to be that of a heart / In the shape of a guitar!   *Repeat*

DA JANELA DO MEU QUARTO

From The Window Of My Room

António Vilar da Costa / Nóbrega e Sousa

THIS ENCHANTING *fado* was made popular by one of the most beautiful voices in *fado* during the mid-20th Century, Tristão da Silva. Da Silva was one of those singers of *fado* who could have had a successful singing career anywhere in the world. Manuel Martins Tristão da Silva was born in Lisbon in 1928 and, as is the case with many of the great *fadistas*, he began singing *fado castiço* as a child of nine during matineé performances in various *fado* clubs, among which was the very popular *'Café Mondego'*. It was in this manner that the young *fadistas*-to-be, usually from the poorer districts of Lisbon, served their apprenticeship.

During this period his talent was noted and he was offered a contract to make a series of recordings, among which were several that achieved great popularity, the most well known probably was *'Nem ás Paredes Confesso'* (Not Even To The Walls Do I Confess).

Tristão da Silva's professional career was thus launched definitively. With his captivating voice and personal style and delivery, other hits rapidly followed: *'Da Janela do Meu Quarto'* (From The Window Of My Room), *'Aquela Janela Virada Pró Mar'* (That Window Facing The Sea), *'Lisboa é Sempre Lisboa'* (Lisbon Is Always Lisbon) and many others.

Although he made numerous recordings during his entire career, there are very few filmed or taped interviews by da Silva chiefly because of the fact that he was afflicted with a stutter so profound that it was hard for him to express himself orally, particularly when he was nervous. In spite of this speech defect, once on stage or in front of a microphone, he performed flawlessly.

Da Silva undertook a number of tours centred in Brazil, but which took him to all parts of South America. After touring for four years, at the insistence of his son Vasco, da Silva returned to Portugal and again undertook a series of concerts and *fado* club appearances. He was also a fine amateur Portuguese guitarist. Tragically, in the prime of his career, da Silva lost his life in a fatal road accident, returning one night from a *fado* club.

'Da Janela do Meu Quarto' is one of the innumerable *fados* that represent musical tributes to Lisbon, and is one of many whose lyrics seem to provide a musical tour of the city. They reveal, for example, that Lisbon, like Rome, is built upon seven hills. What is not entirely clear is whether the lyrics, in speaking of seeing 'the light in her room', are referring to an actual lover or whether the reference is again an allegorical one, i.e. referring, once again, to Lisbon.

One of the most beautiful voices in fado during the mid-20th Century

◀ Tristão da Silva. His exceptional voice and distinctive style made him one of the most acclaimed performers of his time.

DA JANELA DO MEU QUARTO

1. Da jan - e - la do meu quar - to ve - jo a luz do quar-to
(Verse 2 see block lyric)

de - la,_____ quan-do a lu - a vem brin - car_____

nos tel - ha - - dos da vie - la_____

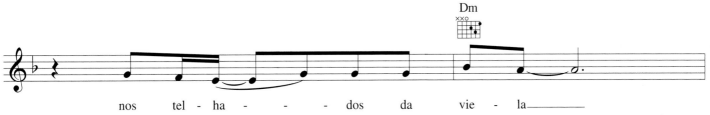

ve - jo o sol_____ de ma-dru - gada a bei - jar_____ sete col-

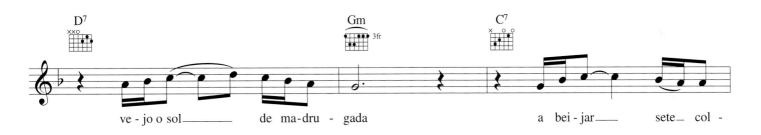

- i - nas_____ qua - ndo se esprai - a no cais - -

- par - a esprei - tar as var - i - nas._____

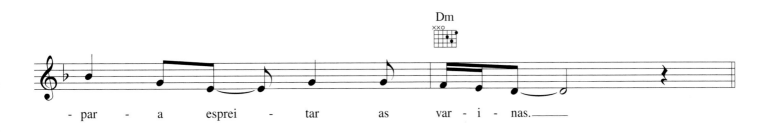

Ve - jo a ron - da la pas - sa a cor - rer,___

vejo a Sé onde à tar - din - ha, com - fer - vor,

el - a vai___ sem - pre___ rezar.

1 Da janela do meu quarto vejo a luz do quarto dela,
   Quando a lua vem brincar nos telhados da viela
   Vejo o sol de madrugada a beijar sete colinas
   Quando se espraia no caispara espreitar as varinas.

   Refrain
   Da janela do meu quarto vejo o mundo
   Tenho um mundo de poesia para ver,
   Vejo Alfama que labuta com ardor, a sorrir e a cantar.
   Vejo o Tejo a espreguiçar-se lá no fundo.
   Vejo a ronda que passa a correr,
   Vejo a Sé onde à tardinha, com fervor,
   Ela vai sempre rezar.

2 Vejo pares de namorados, almas cheias de ilusões
   Toda a magia dum fado, a alegria dos pregões,
   E à noitinha quando as sombras vestem de luto a viela
   Da janela do meu quarto vejo a luz do quarto dela.

   Refrain
   Da janela do meu quarto vejo o mundo
   Tenho um mundo de poesia para ver,
   Vejo Alfama que labuta com ardor, a sorrir e a cantar.
   Vejo o Tejo a espreguiçar-se lá no fundo.
   Vejo a ronda que passa a correr,
   Vejo a Sé onde à tardinha, com fervor, } *Repeat*
   Ela vai sempre rezar.

From the window of my room I see the light of hers,
When the moon comes to play on the rooftops of the alley
Early in the morning I see the sun kiss the seven hills
When it spreads on the wharf to spy on the *varinas*

Refrain
From the window of my room I see the world
I have the world of poetry to see
I see the Alfama as it works hard, smiling and singing
I see the Tagus stretching below
I see the patrol on their rounds, running by
I see the Cathedral where she always goes to pray, ardently,
In the late afternoon

I see couples in love, souls full of illusions
All of the magic of a *fado* and the cheerfulness of the vendors
And at night, when the shadows dress the alleys in mourning
From the window of my room, I see the light in her room.

Refrain
From the window of my room I see the world
I have the world of poetry to see
I see the Alfama as it works hard, smiling and singing
I see the Tagus stretching below
I see the patrol on their rounds, running by
I see the Cathedral where she always goes to pray, ardently,
In the late afternoon

From the window of my room
I see the world
I have the world of poetry to see

A MODA DAS TRANÇAS PRETAS

Black Braids Style

Vicente da Câmara / *Fado Ginguinhas*

ALTHOUGH *FADOS* are usually thought of as sad, passionate creations, full of pathos – and justifiably so – they do not all fall into that vein. Although it is unusual to find *fados* containing any real humour, it is less rare to find a whimsical, lightly nostalgic *fado* and '*A Moda das Tranças Pretas*', which can best be translated as 'Black Braids Style', is one of these.

This song was written by Dom Vicente da Câmara, an important, even revered *fadista* and a member of a noble family that has produced a dynasty of prominent, even illustrious, *fado* singers. Born in Lisbon in 1928, he is a descended from João Zarco da Câmara, a Portuguese navigator who discovered the island of Madeira.

Da Câmara had begun singing early in life and had, as a teacher, an uncle, João Carmo de Noronha, who had made *fado* recordings 20 years previously, in the earliest days of the recording industry. His aunt was the greatly beloved exponent of *fado castiço*, Maria Teresa de Noronha.

The young singer, at 20 years of age, won first prize at the *Fado* Tournament sponsored by Portuguese National Radio, and was invited to perform on radio on a regular basis. He was soon induced to begin recording. Since that time Câmara has performed anywhere in the world where a Portuguese audience exists, including all of Europe, China and Africa. Dom Vicente da Câmara is a singer who remains loyal to the traditional *fado*, old *fado castiço*, or pure *fado*.

In 1989 Vicente de Câmara celebrated his 40th year as a *fadista* in a grand concert in Lisbon in which his son, José da Câmara, the youngest member of the dynasty, participated. José is now a well-established *fadista* in his own right. Dom Vicente's nephew, Nuno da Câmara Pereira, is also a very fine singer: a very popular figure in the world of *fado,* and there are other members of this prominent *fado* family currently performing as well.

Vicente da Câmara is known more for his singing than for his many compositions. '*A Moda das Tranças Pretas*' is the most popular of his compositions, the melody of which is that of a *ginguinhas*. This melody is one of those classic forms to which many lyricists and *fadistas* set their own words. It is named, according to several sources, for a *fado* singer who was active during the last years of the 19th Century. We know this by references made by other singers of the period to having performed with Ginguinhas. It is highly possible that this singer, himself, created this melodic form. '*A Moda das Tranças Pretas*' is the most celebrated of the *fados* sung as a *ginguinhas*. It has continued to remain extremely popular over the years, both with *fadistas* and with their audiences. The recording of this song included herein is one performed by both Don Vicente da Câmara and his son, José.

The Chiado section of Lisbon is the city's oldest and most famous shopping district. It is the place where generations have gone to buy clothing, shoes, jewellry and other fineries as well as music and books. The Chiado, in the days before malls, was the place to see and be seen and where flower girls and other street vendors could always be found.

▲ An early photo of Don Vicente da Câmara. A renowned – even revered – performer, he is also a member of a prominent family of the *fado*.

A MODA DAS TRANÇAS PRETAS

1. Com - o era lin - da, com seu ar nam-ora - deiro
(Verse 3 see block lyric)

'Té lhe cha - ma - vam «men-ina das tranças pre - t - as».

Do Chi - a -do cam - inha - va o dia in - tei - ro

A - pre-goan - do ram - in - hos de vio - le - - tas

Do Chi - a do camin - ha - va o dia in teir - o

A - pre-goan - do ram - in - hos de vi - o - le - tas.

2. E   as rapa - i - - - gas de al - ta ro - - - da que
(Verse 4 see block lyric)

passavam   Fi - ca - vam   tristes____   a pen -

- sar   no   seu   ca - be - lo.   Quando ela ol - ha - - va,   com ver -

To Coda ⊕

- gonha   dis - far - ça - - vam   E   pouco a   pouco____   to - das deixar-

- am   cresc - ê - lo.   Quando ela ol - ha - va,____   con ver -

- gonha   dis - far - çavam   E   pouco a   pouco____

D.C. al Coda

____   to - das   deix - ar - am   cres - cê - - lo.

80

1 Como era linda, com seu ar namoradeiro,
'Té lhe chamavam, «menina das tranças pretas».
Do Chiado caminhava o dia inteiro
Apregoando raminhos de violetas } Repeat

2 E as raparigas d'alta roda que passavam
Ficavam tristes a pensar no seu cabelo.
Quando ela olhava, com vergonha disfarçavam
E pouco a pouco todas deixaram crescê-lo. } Repeat

3 Passaram dias e as meninas do Chiado
Usavam tranças enfeitadas com violetas.
Todas gostavam do seu novo penteado
E assim nasceu a moda das tranças pretas! } Repeat

4 Da violeteira já ninguém hoje tem lembranças.
Deixou saudades, foi-se embora e à tardinha,
Está o Chiado carregado com mil tranças
Mas tranças pretas ninguém tem como ela tinha! } Repeat

How beautiful she was with her coquettish air
They called her the "girl with the black braids"
Through the Chiado she would walk all day long
Crying, "buy a bouquet of violets!"

And the high-class girls that passed
Were saddened when thinking of their hair.
When she glanced back at them bashfully, they
Looked the other way
And, little by little, they all let their hair grow

The days passed and the girls from the Chiado
Began wearing long tresses adorned with violets
They all loved their new hair fashion
And thus was born the style of the black braids

Of the flower girl there remains not even a memory
She departed, leaving only *saudade* behind, and, in
The late afternoon,
Chiado is filled with a thousand braids,
But black braids like hers – no one can find!

JÚLIA FLORISTA

Júlia The Flower Girl

Leonel Vilar / Joaquim Pimentel

THIS POPULAR, non-traditional *fado* is included here because of its great popularity with *fadistas*. It has been included for generations in the recordings of a number of prominent performers, and is still to be found in the repertoires of many singers currently performing in *fado* houses throughout Lisbon. As for its origins, there was, in point of fact, a popular *fadista* who did perform under the name 'Júlia Florista' during the early 1900s, and it is likely that the song was named for her.

The statement, at the end of the first verse, that Júlia 'would sell her flowers, but would never sell her love', is a particularly significant one. The female street vendors of Lisbon, ubiquitous for centuries in all parts of the city, often had a questionable reputation. To add to this, until the end of the 19th Century, *fadistas,* both male and female, often bore unsavoury reputations, similar to the reputations that actors and actresses enjoyed in England and the United States, as well as in Portugal, in the early days of the theatre.

The middle and upper classes considered *fadistas* to be colourful but fascinating thieves – low-life characters on the edge of, often part of, the underworld. The term '*fadista*' became synonymous with 'ruffian' and women singers were often described as 'actresses', and occasionally as outright 'ladies of the evening'. This reputation was occasionally earned but very often unjustified. The public's opinion of *fadistas* was very much altered for the better as it gradually became accepted by the middle classes and even the nobility and members of these classes themselves became *fado* performers.

Since *fado*, although a meeting ground between the upper and lower classes in its popularity, was essentially a social expression of the common people, it tended to express, in many of its lyrics, great empathy for the plight of the urban poor and the working class. There were innumerable songs produced that described, in admiring and sympathetic terms, the poor but noble-hearted working girl, alone and on her own.

This recording of '*Júlia Florista*' by the celebrated *fadista* who was known simply by the name of Max (see '*A Rosinha dos Limões*', earlier) is one of the most popular of this particular *fado*.

▶ The accomplished young *fadista* Misia. Rising from its unsavory reputation in its early days, *fado* came to be appreciated by all classes of Lisbon society.

There were innumerable songs produced that described the poor but noble-hearted working girl, alone and on her own

JÚLIA FLORISTA

1. A Jú-li-a Flo-ris-ta,___ bo-émi-a fad-is-ta, diz a tra-di-
*(Verse 2 see block lyric, 3 Instrumental to *)*

-ção, foi___ nessa Lis-bo-a, fig-u-ra de pro-

-a, da nos-sa can-ção, fi-gu-ra bi-zar-

-ra, que ao som da gui-tar-ra, o fa-do vi-veu.___ Ven-di-a as

flo-res mas os seus a-mor-es jam-ais os ven-deu. Ó Júl-ia

Flor-is-ta, tua lin-da hist-ór-i-a,___ que o tem-po mar-

-cou___ na nos-sa mem-ór-i-a,___ Ó Júl-ia

Flor-ist - a, tu - a voz e - co - a nas noit - es bair-
-rist - as, bo - ém-ias, fa - dist - as da nos-sa Lis - bo - a. 2. Chi - ne - la do
Nas noi-tes bairr-is - tas, bo-ém-ias, fad-ist - as da nos - sa Lis-bo - a.
Nas noi-tes bairr-is - tas, bo-ém-ias, fad-ist - as da nos - sa Lis-bo - a.

1 A Júlia Florista, boémia fadista,
  Diz a tradição,
  Foi nessa Lisboa, figura de proa,
  Da nossa canção,
  Figura bizarra
  Que ao som da guitarra,
  O fado viveu.
  Vendia as flores
  Mas os seus amores
  Jamais os vendeu.

2 Chinela do pé, um ar de ralé
  No jeito de andar.
  Se a Júlia passava, Lisboa parava
  Para a ouvir cantar.
  Falando de amores
  No ar o pregão,
  Na boca a canção,
  E encostada ao peito
  A graça e o jeito,
  Do cesto das flores.

  Refrain
  Ó Júlia Florista, tua linda história,
  Que o tempo marcou
  Na nossa memória,
  Ó Júlia Florista, tua voz ecoa
  Nas noites bairristas, boémias, fadistas
  Da nossa Lisboa.

Júlia the flower girl, an enchanting *fadista*,
So says tradition
In Lisbon she was a proud singer of our song
A singular figure that lived the *fado* to the sound of the guitar
She would sell her flowers, but she never sold her love

With slippers on her feet, she walked with a commonplace air
But if Júlia walked by, Lisbon would stop to hear her sing of love
In the air a street chant, in her mouth a song
And gracefully held to her breast, a basket of flowers

Refrain
Júlia the flower girl, time has implanted your
Beautiful story in our memory
Júlia the flower girl, your voice echoes
Through the haunting *fado* nights of our Lisbon

O PAGEM

Alfredo Rodrigues Duarte / Fernando Teles

The Page Boy

ONE GROUP OF *fado*s, described by the Portuguese as *'fado castiço'* takes as its subject matter the deeply traditional aspects of Portuguese culture, such as the sovereigns, the aristocracy, and noble pursuits such as warfare, courtly love and bullfighting. As described in the Introduction, the word *castiço* comes from the same Latin root as the English word 'caste'. The term *'Fado castiço'* is best translated as 'pure *fado'*. This song is an fine example of this form of Lisbon *fado*.

Alfredo Marceneiro, one of this *fado*'s composers and the *fadista* with whom it is most closely identified, is one of the most important, interesting, and enduring figures in the history of *fado*. Marceneiro was born Alfredo Duarte about the beginning of the last century. His trade was that of master carpenter, or 'marceneiro', a trade that is very highly respected in Portugal, and that honorific became the name by which he was known throughout his life. Marceneiro had a career as a *fadista* and as a writer of great *fados* that spanned more than 40 years.

For some reason Marceneiro recorded only rarely. In fact, after recording in the year 1929 and again in 1936, 35 years elapsed before he made any new recordings. During that interval the contributions of 'Uncle Alfredo', as his awe-stricken colleagues knew him, kept him at the pinnacle of fame and prestige.

Marceneiro had a great ability to synthesise so effectively as to be able to relate an entire story, poignantly and poetically, in three or four short verses. Although this is not his most popular *fado*, it is one of his most dramatic and conveys the impression that it might have been created centuries earlier. Marceneiro recorded this song when he was quite old and it was especially moving when delivered with his dramatic style in his plaintive, high-pitched, voice.

This particular recording of *'O Pagem'* is also enhanced by a superior group of accompanists, among whom are the great Portuguese guitarists Carvalinho and Antonio Chaino.

▲ Alfredo Marceneiro or "Uncle Alfredo" as he was known to his fellow *fadistas*. For many decades he was one of the greatest writers of *fado*, as well as one of the genre's most popular performers.

Marceneiro recorded this song when he was quite old and it was especially moving when delivered with his dramatic style in his plaintive, high-pitched, voice.

O PAGEM

♩= 96

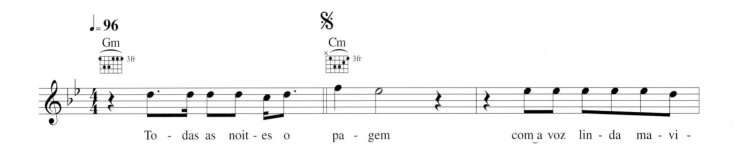

To - das as noit - es o pa - gem com a voz lin - da ma - vi -

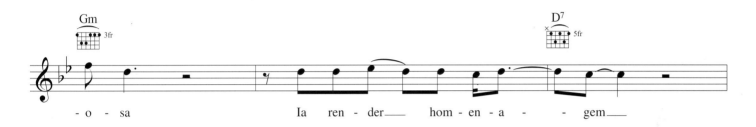

-o - sa Ia ren - der___ hom - en - a - gem___

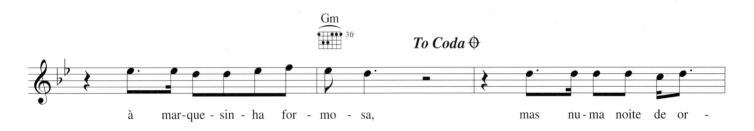

To Coda ⊕

à mar - que - sin - ha for - mo - sa, mas nu - ma noite de or -

- gul - ho o Mar - quês fe - ro, bo - çal,___

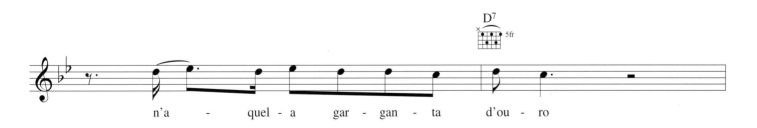

n'a - quel - a gar - gan - ta d'ou - ro

man - dou cra - var um pun - hal. A Mar - que - sa de - lir - an -

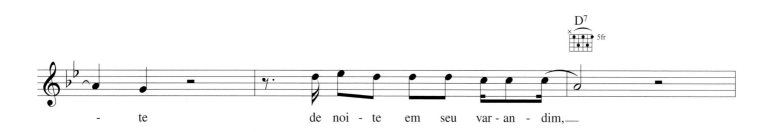

- te de noi - te em seu var - an - dim,—

pobre lou - ca alu - ci - nan - te chor - ando can - tava as -

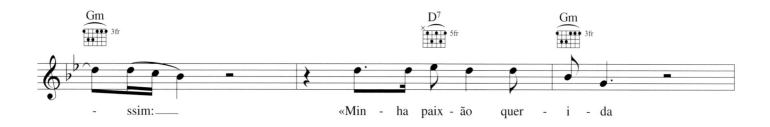

- ssim:— «Min - ha paix - ão quer - i - da

meu a - mor—— meu pa - gem be - lo

rit.

fo - ge sem - pre min - ha vi - da, fo - ge sem - pre min - ha vi -

a tempo · · · · · · · · · · · · · · · · · · · *D.%. al Coda*
(Instrumental)

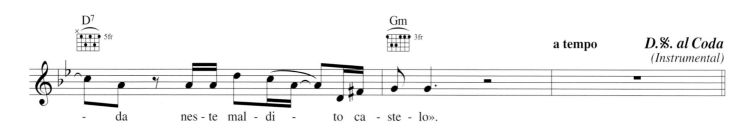

- da nes - te mal - di - to ca - ste - lo».

⊕ *Coda*

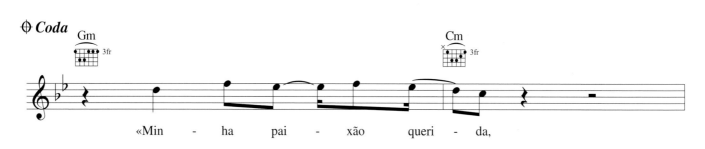

«Min - ha pai - xão queri - da,

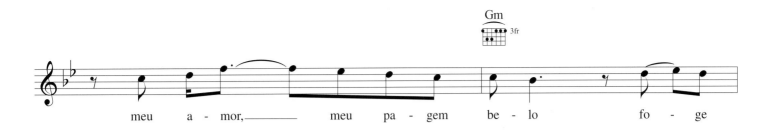

meu a - mor,_____ meu pa - gem be - lo fo - ge

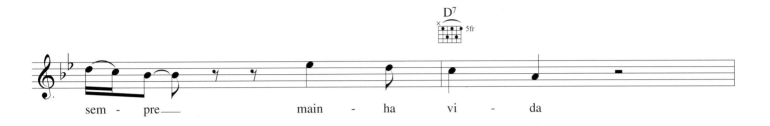

sem - pre____ main - ha vi - da

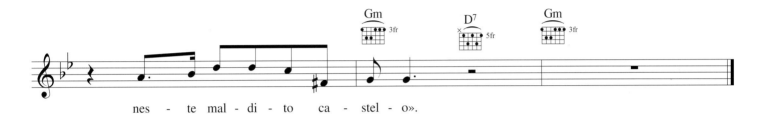

nes - te mal - di - to ca - stel - o».

1   Todas as noites o pagem
    Com a voz linda maviosa
    Ia render homenagem
    À marquesinha formosa,
    Mas numa noite de orgulho
    O Marquêsfero, boçal,
    N'aquela garganta d'ouro
    Mandou cravar um punhal.

2   A Marquesa delirante
    De noite em seu varandim,
    Pobre louca alucinante
    Chorando, cantava assim:
    "Minha paixão querida, meu amor, meu pagem belo
    Foge sempre minha vida, foge sempre minha vida
    Neste maldito castelo."

Each night the page boy,
With his beautiful, sweet voice
Rendered homage
To the lovely young Marquesa
But one arrogant night
The Marquis, in brutish ferocity,
Placed a dagger
In that golden throat

The Marquesa, delirious, on her veranda
Poor crazed woman, hallucinating,
Weeping, singing these words:
"My dear passion, my love, my beautiful page boy
Forever wasting my life, wasting my life
In this cursed castle."

My dear passion, my love,
my beautiful page boy
Forever wasting my life,
wasting my life
In this cursed castle

BONS TEMPOS

Good Times

Joaquim Frederico de Brito / José Galhardo

BONS TEMPOS is another of the non-traditional *fados* popularised by the reknowned Carlos Ramos, whose celebrated hit, '*E Foi-se a Mocidade*', is included earlier in this collection. As mentioned in the Introduction, one of the most popular topics of *fado* is *fado* and the *fadistas* themselves, and this song is a very moving example of this type of lyric. The song is also one that, while reminiscing about the early times of *fado*, also portrays the Lisbon of the distant past nostalgically, and with deep affection.

One of the creators of this *fado,* José Galhardo, was an especially important figure in the development and enrichment of the *fado* during the first half of the 20th Century.

Galhardo, a writer, poet and dramatist, was born in October but the year, either 1905 or 1909, is a matter of dispute. He graduated in law from Lisbon University but began writing poetry and together with other local poets, started involving himself in writing for the theatre. So active and successful did he become in this field that he became Director of the ancient Society of Theatrical Writers and Composers (now the Portuguese Society of Authors).

As a composer of *fados*, Galhardo is responsible for a number of them that are considered among the greatest and most popular of his generation, and future generations as well. For example, Galhardo was the co-writer, with different collaborators, of two of Amália's greatest hits, '*Lisboa Antiga*' and '*Coimbra*', the first two selections in this collection. José Galhardo died in 1967.

The following *fado*, sometimes recorded under the title '*Bons Tempos Antigos*' (Good Old Times), was written for the repertoire of Carlos Ramos and became one of his most popular hits.

The entire song is an homage to a Lisbon of earlier days. The terms *esperas* and *pegas* in the second verse are references to rituals uniquely associated with Portuguese bullfighting. As previously mentioned in discussing '*Lisboa Antiga*', the term *esperas*, or more fully, *esperas de gado,* is an event in which one of the bulls being driven to the bullring is diverted and fought informally, in the streets, by young *aficionados*. *Esperas* literally means 'wait', 'delay', or, as in this case,

'ambush', while the word '*gado*' can be translated as 'cattle' or 'herd'. The participants, both nobles and commoners, traditionally retired together to the nearest tavern to celebrate with food, wine, and *fado* following this event.

Pegas is defined literally as 'grab' or 'catch'. It is used as a noun when referring, as in this instance, to the final stage of the Portuguese bullfight in which a team of men on foot literally challenges the bull to charge them, at which time they receive his charge head on and immobilise him. Some authorities believe this unique custom to be the last living example of the ancient form of bullfighting practised by the Minoans of ancient Crete and illustrated in their art and on their ceramics.

The remainder of the verse refers to reminiscences about the popular street celebrations and fairs during Carnival time when clowns and buffoons would playfully appear carrying large knives and whetstones to frighten the young women, who would obligingly cry out or pretend to faint in surprise. The reference to the '*Avenida*' when used by itself, as in this song, always refers to the *Avenida da Liberdade,* the most important and elegant thoroughfare in Lisbon.

▼ These *forcados* or 'bull-catchers' are part of a team of eight that wrestle bulls and batter their bodies for sheer amusement.

BONS TEMPOS

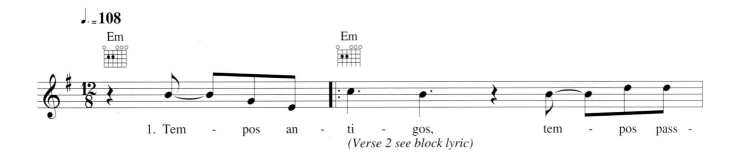

1. Tem - pos an - ti - gos, tem - pos pass -

(Verse 2 see block lyric)

- a - dos, tem - pos ar - tis - tas, tem - pos mor - tos que eu vi -

- vi vel - hos a - mi - gos,___ vel - hos pe -

- ca - dos vel - has fad - i - stas que eu não ve - jo a gora a - qui___

___ Já___ lá vão - to - das, já lá vão

to - dos,___ já lá não fal - ta se não um___ que es - per - a

pas - sou, mor - reu mor - reu,_____ e_____ dess - e

rit.

mun - do que aca-bou fi - quei___ só eu.

1 Tempos antigos, tempos passados,
   Tempos de artistas, tempos mortos que eu vivi
   Velhos amigos, velhos pecados
   Velhas fadistas que eu não vejo agora aqui
   Já lá vão todas, ja lá vão todos
   Já lá não falta se não um que espera vez
   Foram-se as modas, foram-se os modos
   Foi toda a malta do meu tempo com vocês

   Refrain
   Chorai, chorai, por mim, por mim
   Rapaz do tempo que lá vai eu vi no fim,
   Passou passou, morreu, morreu
   E desse mundo que acabou fiquei só eu.

2 Vi as esperas, vi as touradas
   Pegas e tudo no bom estilo português,
   Vi as galeras, vi as cegadas
   O «velho de Entrudo» com desmaios e xexés,
   Vi a Avenida, com luminárias,
   Toda empedrada a preto e branco, sem metro,
   Coisas da vida extraordinárias
   O agora é nada ao pé de tudo o que findou.

   Refrain

Old times, past times, artistic times, long dead
That I lived
Old friends, old sins
Old *fadistas* that I don't see here any more
There they all go,
Excepting only one who awaits his time
Styles changed, fashions departed,
And my old crowd went with them

Refrain
Cry, cry for me
Child of the times that have gone and will not return
Past, past and dead
And of that world that ended, only I remain

I saw the *esperas*, I saw the bullfights,
Pegas and all in good Portuguese style
I saw the floats, I saw the buffoons
An old fashioned Carnival with pranks and jokes
I saw the *Avenida* lit with festival lights
All paved in black and white, even before the Metro
Extraordinary things in life
That today one can no longer find.

Cry, cry for me
Child of the times that have gone
and will not return
   Past, past and dead
And of that world
      that ended,
only I remain

FADO DA DEFESA

Fado Of Defesa Street

António Calém / José António Sabrosa

THIS *FADO* IS A particular favourite of mine because I find the melody of the verse, and the instrumental interval between stanzas, hauntingly beautiful. The lyrics also hold their own as poignant romantic poetry.

The song is also of particular interest because of the seemingly incomprehensible title. The word *defesa* is usually translated as 'defence', 'protection', 'bulwark', etc. It can also be translated as 'forbidden'. In any event, the meaning remained obscure until a reference to the song was found in an old collection that listed the title as *Fado da Rua Defesa*, or 'Fado of Defesa Street'. This went a long way towards clarifying the matter. It became apparent that the song was named for a street in the old part of Lisbon, one which may itself have been so designated because it made up part of a city or castle wall or fortification.

The melody of this particular *fado* was composed by a nobleman, a well-known writer of *fados,* José António Serôdio, the Count of Sabrosa, usually referred to as José Antonio Sabrosa. He wrote it for his wife, the great *fadista* Maria Teresa de Noronha, and it was she who first popularised it. The lyrics are by an eminent poet and lyricist, António Cálem. More recently, *Fado da Defesa* has been included in the repertoire of a number of prominent *fadistas,* among them, Luz Sá da Bandeira and Margarida Bessa.

Luz Sá da Bandeira, a very attractive, statuesque singer with a compelling voice, is currently a popular *fadista* in Lisbon with a considerable following, and can be seen performing at a number of the finest *adegas típicas.* She is featured, together with a number of other *fado* artists, in a multi-volume series of videos on the world of *fado* entitled *Noites de Fado (Fado Nights),* and has also recorded with marked success.

Margarida Bessa is one of the more contemporary group of *fadistas* that have taken older *fados,* both traditional and non-traditional, and succeeded in reinterpreting them, while adhering to the feeling and structure of the originals. Imbuing them with her own personality, Bessa's love for these old songs is clearly demonstrated. It is her interpretation of this classic which is presented on the accompanying CD.

Born in Lisbon, Bessa earned a degree in Germanic studies, and, as is common with a number of *fado* artists, started out by singing only among friends. In her case some of them sent a home-made tape of one of her amateur performances to a *fado* tournament promoted by RTP, the Portuguese Television Network. Bessa made it to the finals and, in a tie-breaker, was awarded second place. Since then her progress as a professional *fadista* has been remarkable. Bessa has been compared stylistically with Maria Teresa de Noronha, but she is in no way imitative of her. Her recordings have met with great success and earned her much respect from lovers of *fado.* Her CD, entitled simply *FADO,* recorded several years ago, contains 'Fado da Defesa' together with her interpretation of a number of other classic and traditional *fados.*

◀ Margarida Bessa, a contemporary *fadista* who has been particularly successful in reinterpreting classic and traditional *fados.*

FADO DA DEFESA

1. Lem - bras-te da nos-sa ru - a que ho - je é a minha, já foi
(Verse 2 see block lyric)

tu - a, tal - ha - da pa - ra nós dois,

foi a - ber - ta pela a - miz - a - de con - stru - í - da com sa - u -

- da - de p'rò a - mor mor - ar de - pois

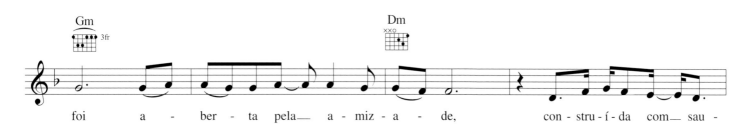

foi a - ber - ta pela a - miz - a - de, con - stru - í - da com sau -

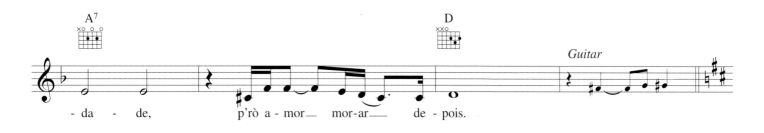

- da - de, p'rò a - mor mor - ar de - pois.

3. Cer - tas noites o lu - ar   tra - ça— o cam-in - ho do mar—

par - a che-gar - es a - té   mim,_____   mas é_____ tão

lon - ga a— a   via - gem,   que só te ve - jo em— mir - a - gem

100

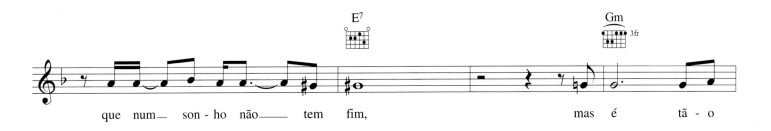

que num— son - ho não—— tem fim,   mas é   tã - o

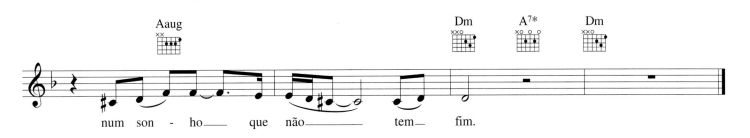

lon - - g a vi - a - gem   que só te vejo em mir - a - gem

num son - ho—— que não———— tem— fim.

1	Lembras-te da nossa rua		Do you remember our street
	Que hoje é a minha, já foi tua,		That today is mine and once was yours,
	Talhada para nós dois,		Carved for the two of us,
	Foi aberta pela amizade,		It was opened by friendship
	Construída com saudade,	*Repeat*	Built with *saudade*
	P'rò amor morar depois.		Where love was later to dwell.

2	Mas um dia tu partiste,		But one day you left,
	E um vento frio e triste		And a cold and sad wind
	Varreu toda a Primavera,		Swept away the spring.
	E agora é o Outono		And now fall came,
	E as folhas ao abandono	*Repeat*	And the abandoned leaves
	Morreram à tua espera.		Died, waiting for you.

3	Certas noites o luar		Some nights the moonlight
	Traça o caminho do mar		Traces an ocean path
	Para chegares até mim,		For you to return to me.
	Mas é tão longa a viagem		But the voyage is so long,
	Que só te vejo em miragem	*Repeat*	That I only see you as a mirage
	Num sonho que não tem fim.		In a dream that never ends.

Some nights the moonlight
                                   Traces an ocean path
For you to return to me

                But the voyage is so long,
                    That I only see you as a mirage
In a dream that never ends

LISBOA NÃO SEJAS FRANCESA

Lisbon, Don't Be French

José Galhardo / Raul Ferrão

FAR FROM BEING derived from a 19th Century ballad, this spirited *fado*, based upon a profoundly important historical event, was actually written in the early 1950s for a musical show (or light opera) entitled *A Invasão* (The Invasion). This musical, which was performed at one of the popular Lisbon theatres, took as its theme that period in history (1807-10) when Portugal was occupied by a foreign invader: Napoleonic France.

'*Lisboa Não Sejas Francesa*' is another of the enduring *fado* hits made popular by the winning combination of the composing efforts of the brilliant José Galhardo, whose collaborator on this song, as on '*Coimbra*', was the fine writer Raul Ferrão, and the vocal magic of the illustrious Amália Rodrigues. Another of their beautiful and very popular *fados* is '*Rosa Enjeitada*' which is often associated with the great *fadista* Maria Teresa de Noronha, and which is presented earlier in this book.

Raul Ferráo, a highly interesting individual indeed, was the composer of some of the finest popular songs as well as *fados* and marches. What makes him particularly unusual was that he was actually trained in chemical engineering and for a military career; and in 1907, at the age of 17 he did, in fact, enter the military. By the middle of World War I, in 1917-18, he was serving as a professor at the School of War in the capital.

Ferrão began composing during the 1920s. Extraordinarily productive as a writer he was later to become a representative of the progenitor of the Portuguese Society of Authors. His music continued to be popular to succeeding generations of Portuguese and in the 1940s alone he is known to have created for nearly 40 shows and reviews. The other of Raul Ferrão's most enduring songs, the ever-popular '*Coimbra*', one of the only two *fados* to become hits in the United States when introduced by the incomparable Amália Rodrigues under the title 'April In Portugal'. As mentioned in our discussion of '*Coimbra*', that song only became a hit later, as a result of Amália's interpretation of it, and Ferrar lived to see world-wide acceptance of his erstwhile rejected song before his death in 1953.

Although '*Lisboa Não Sejas Francesa*' was first performed by one of the stars of '*A Invasão*', Mirita Casimiro, it was later performed and recorded by Amália with tremendous success. The piece has been considered a *fado* classic ever since.

As is the case with a number of previously discussed *fados*, the lyrics utilise the device of picturing Lisbon as a beautiful, but capricious young girl, in this case portraying Portugal itself as an old doting father.

In admonishing 'young lady Lisbon', the singer is cautioning the young women of Lisbon, who were undoubtedly bedazzled by the uniforms and sophistication of the young French officers. The song beseeches them to resist the occupier's charms and to remember their own valiant, but vanquished young men. It begs them to remember that "you are Portuguese, you belong only to us."

The term '*alfacinha*' literally means a small head of lettuce, but can also be translated as 'lettuce eater', which is an affectionate idiomatic term for a citizen of Lisbon. It refers to the fact that, in past times, Lisbonites often dined daily on lettuce that they cultivated on the hillsides and in the private gardens of the city.

◄ A Portuguese fishing boat along the banks of the Rio Tejo (Tagus River) at Lisbon.

LISBOA NÃO SEJAS FRANCESA

1. Não nam-or-es os fran - ce - ses Men - i - - na Lis -
(Verse 2 see block lyric)

- bo - a,_____ Por - tu - gal é mei - go às vez - es mas

cer - tas co - i - sas nã - o per - do - a. Vê - te bem no es - pelho

Desse hon - ra - do vel - ho, Co - mo o teu ex - em - plo a - trai... Vai!

a tempo

segue o seu le - al con - sel - ho, Não dês des-go-st-os ao te - u pai. Lis -

- bo - a não___ se-jas fran - ce - sa, come___ to-da___ a cert - eza não vais ser fe - liz,_

Lis - bo - a que___ i - deia dan - in - ha vai - dos - sa al - fa - cin - ha ca - sar com Par - is. Lis - bo - a, tens___ cá na - mor - ados que diz - em coi - ta - dos com as al - mas na voz: «Lis - bo - a, não___ se - jas fran - ce - sa tu és___ Port - u - gue - sa, tu és só - p'ra___ nós.»

nós.»

Instrumental

O Lis -

-bo - a, tens— nam-or-ados—— que— diz-em coi-tados com-as al - mas na voz: «Lis -

-bo - a, nã-o se - - - - jas fran-ce - sa, tu és por-tu-gue -

- sa, tu és só p'ra—— nós.»

1 Não namores os franceses
   Menina Lisboa,
   Portugal é meigo às vezes
   Mas certas coisas não perdoa.
   Vê-te bem no espelho,
   Desse honrado velho,
   Como o teu exemplo atrai…
   Vai ! segue o seu leal conselho,
   Não dês desgostos ao teu pai.

   Refrain
   Lisboa, não sejas francesa,
   Com toda a certeza
   Não vais ser feliz,
   Lisboa, que ideia daninha,
   Vaidosa alfacinha
   Casar com Paris.
   Lisboa , tens cá namorados
   Que dizem coitados
   Com as almas na voz:
   «Lisboa, não sejas francesa,
   Tu és portuguesa,
   Tu és só p'ra nós.»

2 Tens amor às lindas fardas
   Menina Lisboa,
   Vê lá bem p'ra quem te guardas,
   Donzela sem recato enjoa.
   Tens aí tenentes,
   Bravos e valentes,
   Nados e criados cá…
   Vá, tenha modos mais decentes,
   Menina caprichosa e má.

   Refrain

Don't flirt with the French
Young Miss Lisbon,
Portugal is tender sometimes,
But certain things he does not forgive.
Observe yourself well in the mirror
And see how bad your example is for
Old and honourable Portugal,
Be loyal to him
Lest your father grieve.

Refrain
Lisbon, don't be French
As you will surely
Not be happy,
Lisbon, what a wicked idea
You vain *alfacinha*,
To marry Paris.
Lisbon, you have your own lovers here
Poor unfortunates,
Who soulfully sing:
"Lisbon, don't be French
You are Portuguese
You belong only to us."

We know you love beautiful uniforms
Young Miss Lisbon,
But be careful for whom you wait,
A bold young lady does not please.
There are handsome and valiant lieutenants
Born and raised here,
So act more decently,
You capricious and naughty girl!

*Lisbon, don't be French
You are Portuguese
You belong only to us*

HÁ MUITO QUEM CANTE O FADO

There Are Many Who Sing Fado

Manuel de Almeida / *Fado Corrido*

THE *FADO CORRIDO* is one of the three traditional forms of *fado*. Because the form is up-tempo and often performed in a major key, the lyrics set in this form are frequently lively, often whimsical, in nature and *'Há Muito Quem Cante O Fado'* is an excellent example of the genre.

Although most singers of *fado* can perform in many different genres, they sometimes achieve particular renown in their interpretation of one particular form. One such singer, a compelling performer, was the late Manuel de Almeida. This popular *fadista* was particularly admired for his rendition of *fado corrido* and *fado mouraria*.

Born in the Bairro de Bica district of Lisbon in 1922, Almeida began singing in amateur shows before the age of 15. A shoemaker by trade, his shy disposition led him to perform only as an amateur for many years, not turning professional until he was 29. His first professional engagement was in *'Tipóia'*, a popular restaurant and *fado* venue of the time operated by Adelina Ramos, a well-known *fadista* of the period. Almeida continued to sing at this *fado* house for the next 12 years.

It was not uncommon for *fadistas*, both amateur and professional, to become associated with one particular *adega típica* exclusively for many years and such long-term associations continue to this day. Almeida was no exception and, upon leaving *'Tipóia'*, he began singing at one of the most popular *fado* houses in Lisbon, *'Lisboa a Noite'*, owned by another accomplished *fadista*, Fernanda Maria. Almeida's relationship with this venue lasted 11 years, after which he made his final move and became one of the leading performers at *'Forte Dom Rodrigo'*, a very popular *fado* house in the charming seaside town of Cascais where he remained until his death in 1998. This club was owned by the celebrated *fadista* known simply as Rodrigo, who also performed there. It was during Almeida's tenure at *'Forte Dom Rodrigo'* that I had the privilege of meeting him and seeing him perform on several occasions. Although he spoke no English, he never failed to greet me warmly and enter into conversation in a slow Portuguese for my benefit. Although personally shy and unassuming, his performances were always compelling and he kept his audiences enthralled.

Almeida made relatively few recordings, his career resting mostly on his live performances in the above mentioned *fado* clubs. One recording that is particularly cherished by his admirers is entitled *'Eu Fadista Me Confesso'* (I, Fadista, Confess).

Manuel de Almeida, a gracious and gentle individual, was a fine sportsman and athlete in his youth. Even in his later years, he could often be seen riding his bicycle through the streets of Cascais. His friend Rodrigo lamented, at the time of Almeida's death, that it marked the passing of "one of the last of the great 'old-time' *fadistas*."

As previously stated, the differences between *fado corrido* and *fado mouraria*, lying mostly in the accompaniment, are relatively minor and so subtle as to be distinguishable only to *fadistas, guitarristas* and true *fado* devotees. This entry represents one of Manuel de Almeida's finer *fado corridos*.

There are, in point of fact, two types of *fado corrido*. They are distinguished only by speed, the fast *corrido* being a virtual cascade of clever or humorous words pouring forth at breakneck speed from the throat of the singer. The typical *corrido,* which the following entry represents, while not normally as sedate or mournful as other *fados,* is performed at a normal tempo. Manuel de Almeida was a master at both.

▼ Manuel de Almeida in performance. One of the last of the great 'old-time' *fadistas*.

This popular fadista was particularly admired for his rendition of fado corrido

HÁ MUITO QUEM CANTE O FADO

- is - ta é ter express-ão é sen-tir tu-do o que can - ta, é tra-

- zer o cor-a - çã - o e a al - ma presa à gar - gan - ta. É

rit.

tra - zer o cor-a - ção e a al - ma presa à gar - gan - ta.

Não é fadista quem quer Quando um dia o fado canta, O ser fadista é trazer A alma presa à garganta.	Not everyone is a *fadista* who wants to be, Just because one day they sing a *fado*. To be a *fadista* is to have your soul Tied to your throat.
«Ninguém duvide ninguém,» É do povo este ditado: «Há muito quem cante fado Mas pouco quem cante bem.»	"No one should doubt anyone," Goes an old saying, "There are many who sing *fado* But few who sing it well."
E sou firme, podem crer Neste meu ponto de vista, Fadista nasce fadista Não é fadista quem quer.	And I am firm in this point of view, That you can believe. A *fadista* is born a *fadista*, Not everyone is a *fadista* who wants to be.
Ser fadista é ter expressão É sentir tudo o que canta, É trazer o coração E a alma presa à garganta. } *Repeat*	To be a *fadista* is to have expression To feel everything that is sung. To be a *fadista* is to tie the heart and soul To the throat.

Lisbon then only has
the heart of a soul carried away
Tied to the guitar, she sings
until the dawn

LISBOA É SEMPRE LISBOA

Lisbon Is Always Lisbon

Artur Joaquim de Almeida Ribeiro / Nóbrega e Sousa

THIS CAPTIVATING *fado* became very popular in the mid-1950s and early 1960s as a result of its being recorded by two of *fado*'s finest performers, Carlos Ramos and Tristão da Silva. The recordings of both of these incomparable artists are available and it is fascinating to listen to how each of them makes the song his own.

This *fado* itself was the result of a collaboration between the creative lyricist, Nóbrega e Sousa (who also produced the lyrics for the Tristão da Silva hit '*Da Janela do Meu Quarto*') and the inspired writer Artur Ribeiro, who was responsible for a number of exceptional *fados*.

Here again we see Lisbon, in that apparently most inexhaustible of guises – that of a young girl, working, flirting, laughing and listening to *fado*.

As discussed earlier, the word *varina*, mentioned in the first line of Verse 1, makes reference to an interesting element in the daily life of Lisbon. Female fish vendors were in earlier days to be seen peddling their wares, in baskets on their heads, through the streets of the ancient districts of the city.

In the past, many of these women came traditionally from the little fishing village of Ovar in Northern Portugal, hence the name '*varina*'. *Varinas* were a colourful part of the Lisbon street scene for generations. Not only are they often mentioned in *fados*, but they are the subjects of a number of them as well.

The *Sé* or ancient Cathedral referred to in this song, is one of the historical landmarks of Lisbon. When the great earthquake struck and virtually destroyed Lisbon on Sunday morning, All Saints' Day, November 1, 1755, a large number of the important citizenry and nobility were inside, celebrating Mass. Many people were killed within the structure itself and many thousands more in the city. The *Sé* was left a shell-like ruin throughout the following centuries as a memorial to those who perished. Its impressive arched remains grace the skyline and are particularly beautiful at night, when lit from below.

▼ A performance in a typical *fado* club. Some of the younger singers have abandoned the shawl and a few of them the traditional black; the wearing of a hat, however, is very unusual.

LISBOA É SEMPRE LISBOA

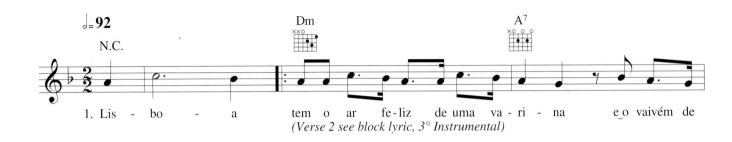

♩=92

N.C.   Dm   A⁷

1. Lis - bo - a   tem o ar fe - liz de uma va - ri - na   e o vaivém de

(Verse 2 see block lyric, 3° Instrumental)

Dm

um - a can - ção em cada es - qu - i - na,   pe - los mer -

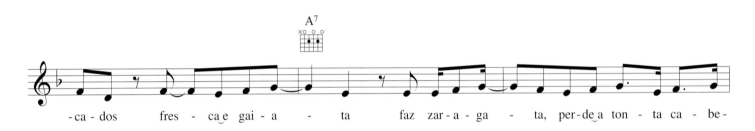

A⁷

-ca - dos fres - ca e gai - a - ta faz zar - a - ga - ta, per - de a ton - ta ca - be -

Dm   A⁷   Dm

-ci - ta.   A - qui e ali na - mora e ri sem vai - da - de, veste___ de chi -

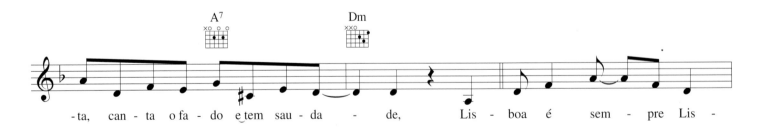

A⁷   Dm

-ta, can - ta o fa - do e tem sau - da - de,   Lis - boa é sem - pre Lis -

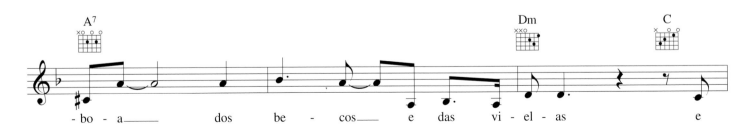

A⁷   Dm   C

-bo - a___   dos be - cos___ e das vi - el - as   e

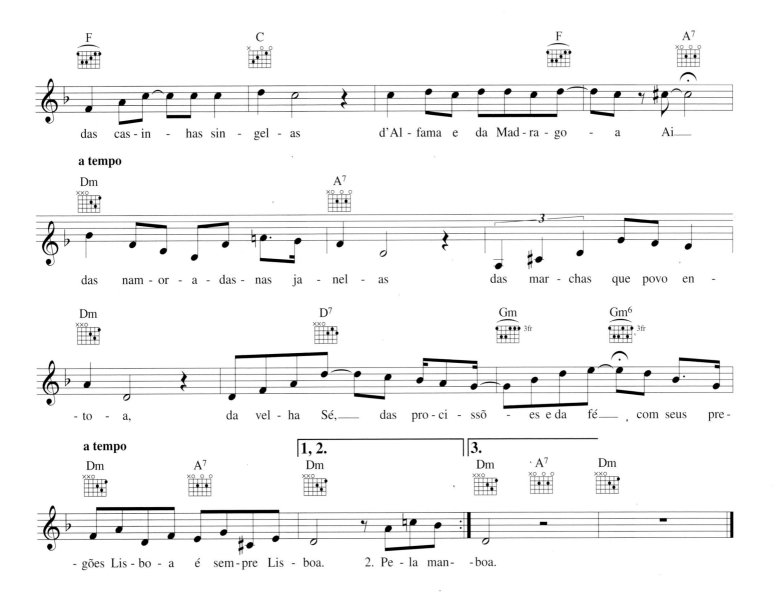

1 Lisboa tem o ar feliz de uma varina
  E o vaivém de uma canção em cada esquina,
  Pelos mercados fresca e gaiata
  Faz zaragata, perde a tonta cabecita.
  Aqui e ali namora e ri sem vaidade,
  Veste de chita, canta o fado e tem saudade.

  Refrain
  Lisboa é sempre Lisboa, dos becos e das vielas
  E das casinhas singelas d'Alfama e da Madragoa,
  Das namoradas nas janelas
  Das marchas que o povo entoa,
  Da velha Sé, das procissões e da fé
  Com seus pregões Lisboa é sempre Lisboa.

2 Pela manhã vai trabalhar toda garrida
  De tarde ao chá Lisboa vive cheia de vida,
  Mas à noitinha olhos rasgados
  Semicerrados na oração mais bizarra,
  Lisboa então só coração de alma levada,
  Presa à guitarra canta até à madrugada.

  Refrain

Lisbon has the happy look of a *varina*
And the coming and going of a song on each corner,
At the markets, lively and playful, she causes uproar,
Loses her foolish little head,
Here and there she flirts and laughs without presumption
She wears chintz, sings the *fado* and feels *saudade*.

Refrain
Lisbon is always Lisbon, of the lanes and alleys
And the simple little houses of Alfama and Madragoa.
Of the lovers at the windows
Of the marches that the people sing,
The old Cathedral , the processions,
The acts of faith, the street vendor's cries,
Lisbon is always Lisbon

In the morning she colourfully goes to work
In the afternoon at tea-time she is full of life,
But at night, with her half-closed eyes, she is exotic,
Lisbon then only has the heart of a soul carried away
Tied to the guitar, she sings until the dawn.

FADO TRINTA E UM

Fado Thirty One

José Maria S. Pereira Coelho / João Alves Coelho

FADO, INEXTRICABLY BOUND as it is to the concept of *saudade*, is justifiably regarded as generally a sad, often tragic music. There are, however, numerous exceptions and this song is one of them. Just as there is a class of songs – *fados castiços* – which reflect the lives of the royalty and nobility, there are *fados* that reflect those of the common people. This particular *fado* is one of the latter; rather than relating a unique or tragic story, it is merely a portrait of the life of ordinary people doing ordinary things. The refrain is totally incomprehensible unless one understands that the term *trinta e um*, (thirty-one) actually has two meanings. Primarily it refers to an early popular card game. The second meaning is that of a ruckus or melee (which meaning evolved, most likely, from the frequent conflicts that probably took place in relation to the primary meaning).

'*Fado Trinta e Um*' is an old *fado*. It was first recorded as early as 1905 by the *fadista* Dona Adelaide Ribeiro and again around 1910. It has continued in the repertoires of various *fadistas* ever since. One of the finest recordings was one made in the 1970s by a noteworthy figure in the world of *fado*, António Mello Corrêa.

Corrêa, born in 1945, was, similar to a number of prominent *fadistas*, from an old noble family and thus entitled to use the honorific 'Dom' before his name. He became intrigued by *fado* at an early age, often skipping classes and slipping out at night to sing in local clubs – conduct that earned him considerable punishment.

Corrêa began his professional career at one of the finest *adegas típicas*, the '*Taverna do Embuçado*', achieving great success and rapidly building a fine reputation. In 1975 Corrêa opened the prestigious *fado* house '*Senhor Vinho*' together with his friends, José Luís Gordo, and the excellent *fadista* Maria da Fé. '*Senhor Vinho*' continues today to be one of the top *fado* houses in Lisbon.

During his career Corrêa was responsible for introducing a number of very popular *fados*. He had great skill in selecting a repertoire that fully displayed his powerful, yet sensitive, expressive voice. His version of '*Tamanquinhas*', the song following '*Fado Trinta e Um*' in this collection, is also particularly fine. Corrêa always dressed in black as he often said he "could not see himself dressed any other way". A

career that would certainly have risen to yet greater heights was tragically cut short by his untimely death in 1982 at the age of 37.

Another very fine rendition of '*Fado Trinta e Um*' was recorded by Carlos Mecedes, a very talented *fadista* who, like Carlos Ramos and to a lesser extent, Tristão da Silva, is very accomplished on the Portuguese guitar and usually accompanies himself, and sometimes other artists on this instrument. Mecedes continues to be a popular and well-respected performer, often appearing at the popular club '*Senhor Vinho*' and occasionally at other venues.

The '*Brasileira*' mentioned in the first line of this song is a reference to a famous coffee house – '*A Brasileira*' – one of Lisbon's landmarks. Existing since the 1800s in the same location in the Chiado, the pedestrian shopping district of Lisbon, it has been, from its beginnings, a meeting place for poets and writers as well as for ordinary Lisbon dwellers. Seated at one of the tables outside the establishment, a spot at which he could often be found, is a bronze statue of the legendary Portuguese poet Fernando Pessoa (see page 129). A number of Pessoa's ballads have been used as lyrics for some of the finest *fados*.

▼ António Mello Corrêa was responsible for introducing a number of very popular *fados* before his untimely death in 1982 at the age of 37.

The 'Brasileira' is a reference to a famous coffee house — one of Lisbon's landmarks

FADO TRINTA E UM

À por - ta da "Bra - sil - ei - ra" dois ti -
- pos en - cont - ram dois. Jun - tam - se os quatro e de - pois
lá co - me - ça a ca - va - queira. A - gra - va - se a chin - frin -
- ei - ra vai aumen - tan - do o zum - zum vem pum re - ben - ta pum. De -
- pois mais tarde ver - eis vinte e qua - tro, vinte e seis, vinte e nove e trin - ta e um. Ai -
- ol - ar - i - lo le - la. Como este não há nen -

- hum. Tu - do bate___ em, Por - tu - gal___ o fa - do trin - ta e um. Ai -

- ol - ar - i - lo le - la___ Como este___ não há nen - hum. Tu - do bate___ em, Por - tu - gal___

___ o fa - do trin - ta e um. um.

1. À porta da "Brasileira" dois tipos encontram dois
Juntam-se os quatro e depois lá começa a cavaqueira
Agrava-se a chinfrineira, vai aumentando o zunzum
Vem pum, rebenta pum
Depois mais tarde vereis
Vinte e quatro, vinte e seis, vinte e nove e trinta e um

Refrain
Aiolarilo lela
Como este não há nenhum } *Repeat*
Tudo bate em Portugal
O fado trinta e um

2. Um homem quer sarilhos por um motivo qualquer
Discute com a mulher e dá porrada nos filhos.
A sogra nos mesmos trilhos para não ficar em jejum
Leva também um fartum. Acaba tudo ao biscoito.
Vinte e quatro, vinte e seis, vinte e nove e trinta e um.

Refrain

3. Já de manhã os tachados bebem fino da botija
Viram dois copos da rija, de quatro em dois separados
Depois de bem engraxados para não ficar em jejum
Tomam dois copos de rum
Vem Carcavelos e Porto e no fim está tudo torto
Arrebenta o trinta e um.

Refrain

Two men meet another two
By the door of the '*Brasileira*'
The four get together and the long chat starts,
As the chat progresses the rumours begin.
A bang leads to another bang,
And then you will hear
Twenty-four, twenty-six, twenty-nine and thirty-one.

Refrain
Aiolarilo lela
There is no *fado* like this one
Everything in Portugal goes well
With the *fado* thirty-one.

A man that for some reason is looking for trouble,
Argues with the wife and beats up the kids.
So the mother-in-law doesn't feel left out,
She also gets part of the stink.
All hell breaks loose,
Twenty-four, twenty-six, twenty-nine and thirty-one.

Refrain

Already early in the morning
The drunks swig liquor from the clay bottle.
They gulp down two glasses of brandy
Four total from two separate ones.
After they are totally smashed,
Not to be on an empty stomach, they drink two glasses of rum
Then comes the Carcavelos and the Port.
And at the end everything is spinning
And the thirty-one bursts out.

Refrain

TAMANQUINHAS

Little Clogs

Joaquim Frederico de Brito

THE TITLE '*Tamanquinhas*', meaning 'little clogs', is one that makes reference to the open-toed wooden clogs typically worn by the *varinas* and other working class women of Lisbon. Another of the innumerable *fados* that represent Lisbon allegorically as a beautiful young woman, *Tamanquinhas* is also one of the many *fados* that are love poems to Lisbon.

The composer of this captivating work, as well as several others in this collection, is one of the most brilliant and prolific folk poets and writers in the history of *fado*, Frederico de Brito. Frequently known by the affectionate diminutive 'Britinho', both the quality and quantity of the body of work left by him are the stuff that legends are made of.

At the age of eight Frederico de Brito started composing verses for his brother to sing at parties. Most people simply did not believe that he had written them until one day, upon hearing an adult poet improvising four-line stanzas, he decided to do the same on the spot, to the amazement of his audience.

Later de Brito himself embarked upon a career as a singer of *fado* while working also as a plasterer and, later, a taxi driver. In 1931, while working at this job, he published a work entitled '*Musa ao Volante*', (Poetry Behind the Wheel). Britinho continued to produce poetry and *fado* throughout his later career as an employee of an oil company; indeed he remained prolific throughout his life. De Brito also wrote several works for the Lisbon theatre. At the time of his death at the age of 85, Frederico de Brito was probably responsible for over a thousand lyrics and several hundred songs.

Recorded by a number of *fadistas*, this version of '*Tamanquinhas*', performed by António Mello Corrêa, is particularly moving.

▼ Popular *fadista* Maria da Fé performing in an ideal setting. Note the mural of performers serving as a backdrop.

*One of the many fados that are
love poems to Lisbon*

TAMANQUINHAS

1. De can - ti - gas e sau - da - des——
(Verses 3&4 see block lyric)

vive—— es - ta lin - da Lis - bo - a,

faz lou - cu - ras e mal - da - des, mas—— no fun - do pu-ra e-bo-

- a nas su - as le - vi - an - da - des.

2. Vive es - ta lin - da Lis - bo - a

dif - eren - te de out - ras ci - da - des,

É Bair-ro Al - to, Ma-dra-go - a de fei - tos—— e qual-i - da-

1 De cantigas e saudades
Vive esta linda Lisboa,
Faz loucuras e maldades,
Mas no fundo pura e boa
Nas suas leviandades

2 Vive esta linda Lisboa
Diferente de outras cidades,
É Bairro Alto, Madragoa
Defeitos e qualidades
Tudo tem esta Lisboa } *Repeat*

3 Burguesinha no Chiado
No seu pátio costureira
Nos retiros canta o fado,
No mercado é regateira
E o Tejo é seu namorado

4 Faz das cantigas pregões
Gosta do sol e da lua
Vai com fé nas procissões,
Doida nas marchas da rua } *Repeat*
Tem ciúmes e paixões.

On songs and *saudades*
Does beautiful Lisbon live,
She is wild and mischievous,
But, after all, pure and good
In her frivolities

This pretty Lisbon lives
Differently from other cities,
It's the Biarro Alto and Madragoa
This Lisbon has both faults and good qualities

She is a city dweller in the Chiado
She is a seamstress in her courtyard
Who sings *fado* at the cafés,
She is a vendor at the street market
And the Tagus is her lover

She turns songs into street cries
She loves the sun and the moon
She goes devotedly to religious processions,
And madly loves the street dancers
She has jealousies and passions.

AH, QUANTA MELANCOLIA

Ah, So Much Sadness

Fernando Pessoa / Alfredo Rodrigo Duarte / *Fado Bailado*

THIS HAUNTING *fado* is written in the style of a *fado bailado*, which is a form attributed to the great Alfredo Marceneiro. Unlike a traditional *fado menor*, which is essentially rhythmless, more like a sombre ballad sung to music accompaniment, the *fado bailado* is played in a pronounced 2/4 rhythm. The descriptive term *bailado* (from *bailar*, to dance) is added because of the swinging or dancing movement it can evoke in the singer and audience.

The lyrics of this particular *fado* are actually from a poem by one of Portugal's greatest poets, Fernando Pessoa. Pessoa was born in Lisbon in 1888 and died there in 1935. He was raised and given an English education in Durban, South Africa, where his stepfather was Portuguese Consul. He returned to Lisbon at the age of 17 and remained there for the next 30 years, where he made a modest living writing letters in English and French for commercial firms. This employment left him much free time to devote to poetry. Pessoa became profoundly influential as a poet; a number of his lyrics were set to music and became popular as *fados*.

Pessoa's passionate lyrics, set to the *fado bailado*, were recently recorded on a CD album by one of the most important new *fadistas* of the current generation, a singer known only as Camané. This excellent young performer is considered by many of his peers to be one of the finest of the newer *fadistas*. On the CD, *Na Linha da Vida* (In The Line Of Life), which contains this poignant ballad, Camané performs *fados* by some of the finest lyricists and poets of both the old and new Portugal.

Camané was introduced to *fado* at the age of seven when, while ill at home, he decided to listen to his father's recordings, which were mainly *fado*. He was exposed to the greatest of the singers of that time, including Maria Teresa de Noronha, Lucíla do Carmo and Carlos do Carmo. He began to perform at private gatherings at the age of 10 and at 12 he won the prestigious 'Great Night of Fado' award.

At the age of 18 Camané began singing at some of Lisbon's finest *fado* houses. He was later frequently booked for concert appearances throughout Europe and he continues to perform in concert widely to this day. When not on tour Camané loves to perform in the small typical *fado* houses still to be found throughout Lisbon's oldest quarters.

While, as mentioned earlier, both the *fado* and *saudade* are often, themselves, the subjects of *fados*, it should be noted that, in reality, the true subject being treated is often that of 'fate' itself – usually a tragic fate that one seeks to endure with what one writer has described as a "quiet desperation". This is clearly the emotion evoked by Pessoa's poignant lyrics in this passionate *fado*.

▼ The excellent young performer, Camané, who is considered by many of his peers to be one of the finest of the newer *fadistas*

▶ Statue of the revered poet Fernando Pessoa seated in front of the famous 'A *Brasileira*' coffee house (see page 120).

The true subject being treated is often that of 'fate' itself

AH, QUANTA MELANCOLIA

1. Ah, quan - ta melan - col - i - a
(Verse 3 see block lyric)

quan - ta, quan - ta sol - i - dã - o,

a - quel - a al - ma que vaz - i - a, que sin - to in - út - il e

fri - a den - tro do me - u cor - a - ção.—

2. Que an - gúst - i - a——— des - es - per - a - da.
(Verse 4 see block lyric)

que— má - go - a que sabe a fim,—

se a nau foi a-ban-don - a - da, e o ce - go caí - 'u—— na es - tra-

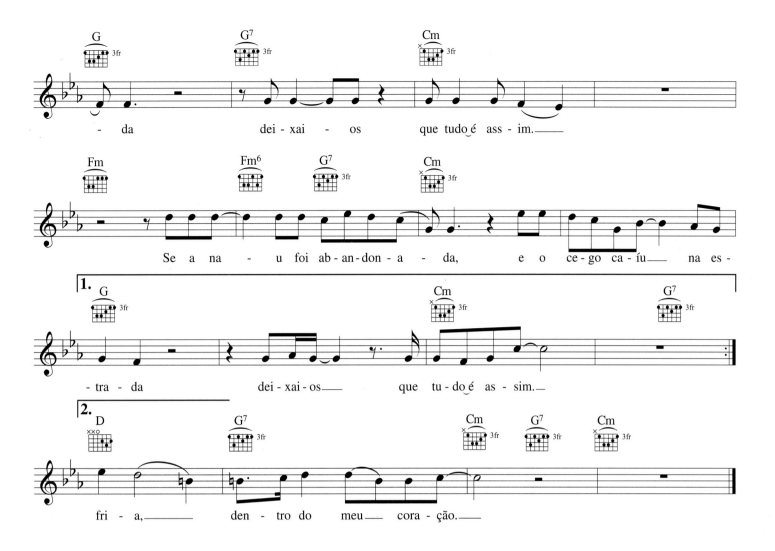

1 Ah, quanta melancolia
   Quanta, quanta solidão,
   Aquela alma que vazia,
   Que sinto inútil e fria
   Dentro do meu coração.

2 Que angústia desesperada
   Que mágoa que sabe a fim,
   Se a nau foi abandonada,
   E o cego caíu na estrada   } Repeat
   Deixai-os que tudo é assim.

3 Sem sossego, sem sossego
   Nenhum momento de meu,
   Onde for que a alma emprego,
   Na estrada morreu o cego
   A nau desapareceu.

4 Ah, quanta melancolia
   Quanta, quanta solidão,
   Aquela alma que vazia
   Que sinto inútil e fria,   } Repeat
   Dentro do meu coração.

So much sadness
So much solitude,
That so empties my soul,
That I feel futile and cold
In my heart.

What a hopeless anguish
What grief that signifies the end,
If the vessel was abandoned,
And the blind man fell on the street
Leave them, for all is as is.

Without rest, without rest
There is not a quiet moment for my soul,
On the street the blind man died
The vessel disappeared.

So much sadness
So much solitude,
That empties my soul
That I feel futile and cold
In my heart.

MARIA MADALENA

Mary Magdelene

Gabriel de Oliveira / Augusto Gil / *Fado Mouraria*

THE *FADO MOURARIA* IS, as previously described, one of the three forms of traditional *fado*, and is named for the ancient Mouraria district of Lisbon, one of the most ancient areas of the city. This song form can be identified by the unique, complex and pulsating guitar accompaniment that can be heard behind the singer. *Fadistas* themselves have been heard to comment that, while any reasonably good *guitarrista* can play a *Fado Menor* or a *Fado Corrido*, it takes a great *guitarrista* to play a *Fado Mouraria* well.

The *Fado Corrido* (running *fado*) and the *Fado Mouraria* are both up-tempo song forms and are used for themes that, while they may be sad, nostalgic or whimsical, are rarely, if ever, the tragic, plaintive ones found in the *Fado Menor*.

'*Maria Madalena*' is a very well-known and much loved version of a *Fado Mouraria* and discographies indicate that it was first recorded on February 1, 1946 by one of the most respected and influential interpreters of *fado*, Lucília do Carmo, the mother of one of this generation's finest *fado* artists, Carlos do Carmo. One of her most popular recordings, she re-recorded '*Maria Madalena*' over 20 years later using improved technology.

Born in Portalegre in 1920, Lucília do Carmo travelled to Lisbon when quite young, where her talents were immediately noticed. She began her professional career at the age of 17 singing in the local *adegas típicas*. Having been noted and recommended by one of the *fado* world's great singers and club managers, Felipe Pinto, she was soon singing at '*A Severa*', a very prominent club. She quickly became one of the most famous performers in Lisbon, singing at various venues until her marriage to Alfredo de Almeida, a local businessman who became her manager and was instrumental in helping her refine her vocal talent.

In 1947 Sr. Almeida opened what was to become a historic *fado* house, first named '*Adega da Lucíla*' and later '*O Faia*'. This club remained one of the most popular and important *fado* clubs in Lisbon, partly because of her performances and partly as a result of the quality performers that she, her husband and, later, her son were able to attract. Among these were illustrious names such as Carlos Ramos, Alfredo

Marceneiro and Tristão da Silva. Upon her husband's early death, the responsibility for management of the club fell upon their son, Carlos, who, as a result, was forced to delay the start of his remarkable career for a number of years. Lucília do Carmo also achieved great popularity in Brazil, where she had made her home for five years.

Lucília had a unique approach to her material. Not one to be described as a soft or dulcet-voiced singer, she approached each song in a direct, honest, but passionately assertive style. A queen of the *fado* in the grand manner, at her club she surrounded herself with some of the great artists of *fado*. It was often her practice, after the last patron had left, to lock the doors and exchange favourite *fados* with her gifted colleagues and friends until the wee hours of the morning.

One writer, describing her career related that, when *fado* lovers went to hear her they wouldn't say they were going to hear *fado*, but that they were "going to Lucília". Lucília do Carmo actively disliked recording studios and the recording process so she did not leave a large record legacy, but those recordings that do exist are generally regarded as classics.

▼ The celebrated Lucília do Carmo, a renowned performer and mother of the incomparable Carlos do Carmo.

MARIA MADALENA

♩ = 126

1. Quem que por a - mor se per-de-u não chore,— não ten-ha pen-a,
(Verses 2-4. see block lyrics)

quem que por a - mor— se per-de-u não— chore, não ten-ha pen-a.

Um-a das San-tas do céu foi— Mar - i - a Mad-a-len - a. 2. Desse a-

Play 4 times

Fez da ma-ior— pe-ca-dor-a um-a das san - tas do céu. 5. E da tan-

- ta que pecou— da mai-or à mas— pe-que-na, E—

— da tan - ta que pe - cou— da mai-or à mas— pe-quen - a ai - a-que-

- la que mais a - mou foi___ Ma - ri - a Ma - da - lena,___ o a-que-

- el - a que mais___ a - mou foi Ma - ri - a___ Ma - da - len - a.

Quem que por amor se perdeu não chore, não tenha pena,
Quemque por amor se perdeu não chore, não tenha pena,
Uma das Santas do céu foi Maria Madalena
Uma das Santas do céu foi Maria Madalena.

Desse amor que nos encanta até Cristo padeceu,
Desse amor que nos encanta até Cristo padeceu,
Para poder tomar santa quem por amor se perdeu
Para poder tomar santa quem por amor se perdeu.

Jesus só nos quis mostrar que o amor não se condena,
Jesus só nos quis mostrar que o amor não se condena,
Por isso quem sabe amar não chore, não tenha pena
Por isso quem sabe amar não chore, não tenha pena.

A Virgem, Nossa Senhora, quando amor conheceu,
A Virgem, Nossa Senhora, quando amor conheceu,
Fez da maior pecadora uma das santas do céu
Fez da maior pecadora uma das santas do céu.

E da tanta que pecou da maior à mas pequena,
E da tanta que pecou da maior à mas pequena,
Ai aquela que mais amou foi Maria Madalena
Aquela que mais amou foi Maria Madalena.

Don't cry or have pity on someone who lost in love
Don't cry or have pity on someone who lost in love
One of the saints of heaven was Mary Magdelene
One of the saints of heaven was Mary Magdelene

The result of that love that delights us even Christ suffered
The result of that love that delights us even Christ suffered
In order to make a saint out of someone who was lost in love.
In order to make a saint out of someone who was lost in love.

Jesus only wanted to show us that you don't condemn love
Jesus only wanted to show us that you don't condemn love
For this reason, he who knows how to love should not cry,
should not feel sorrow.
For this reason, he who knows how to love should not cry,
should not feel sorrow.

When Our Lady, the Virgin, loved,
When Our Lady, the Virgin, loved,
She turned the worst sinner into one of the saints of heaven.
She turned the worst sinner into one of the saints of heaven.

And of all those who have sinned, from the biggest to the smallest,
And of all those who have sinned, from the biggest to the smallest,
The one that loved the most was Mary Magdalene.
The one that loved the most was Mary Magdalene.

MINHA MÃE FOI CIGARREIRA
My Mother Was A Cigarette Maker

Filipe de Almeida Pinto / João Linhares Barbosa / Henrique Lopes do Rego / Francisco Duarte Ferreira / *Fado Menor*

WITH '*MINHA MÃE FOI CIGARREIRA*' (My Mother Was A Cigarette Maker) we come finally to a splendid example of the oldest and most fundamental of the traditional forms of Lisbon *fado*, that most profound and tragic of forms, the *fado menor*.

'*Minha Mãe Foi Cigarreira*' is a very old song. This is an early recording of it by a popular *fadista* of the late 1920s-40s, Filipe Pinto. In 1930, as part of a group representing some of the finest names in *fado*, Pinto was invited to travel to Madrid to make a series of recordings for Odeon records. This song was included among the rare and memorable group of songs recorded at that time.

Pinto was born in 1905 and began singing *fado* at the age of 15. As was the case with most *fadistas*, he began his career as an amateur maintaining various daytime jobs while developing his own particular style of performance in local *fado* houses. He began his professional career at the '*Ferro de Engomar*', one of the most famous of the *fado* houses in the old section of Lisbon during the first half of the 20 Century where many of the finest *fadistas* would launch their careers. From there he proceed to perform at several other very prominent venues, including '*A Severa*' and '*Café Mondego*'.

Around 1946, after years of performing, Pinto replaced one of the greatest of the Portuguese guitarists, Armandinho, as manager and host of an early and very popular *Casa de Fado*, '*Café Luso*'. For this venue Pinto was able to book, over the years, the finest *fadistas* and guitarists who were presented to an audience of the middle and upper classes of Portuguese society as well as to visiting diplomats and tourists. Pinto died in Lisbon in 1968.

This ballad provides an excellent illustration of two of *fado menor*'s persistent themes: motherhood and the dignity of the working classes.

As noted previously, parenthood, especially motherhood, is a traditional subject for *fado*. The Portuguese being a deeply sentimental people, there is an almost mystical depiction of the parent-child relationship.

The Portuguese insist that the *fado menor*, as with the other two forms of traditional *fado*, "has no melody". In other words, the lyrics can be sung to whatever melody is selected by the *fadista,* as long as the traditional chord pattern that is used fits the number of lines in each verse. Having acknowledged that fact, this particular melody remains one of a number that are often chosen for the singing of *fado menor*.

Parenthood, especially motherhood, is a traditional subject for fado

MINHA MÃE FOI CIGARREIRA

1. Min - ha mãe foi cig - arr - ei - ra e tinha um por - te biz - ar - ro,
(Verses 4&5 see block lyric)

Min - ha mãe foi cig - arr - ei - ra e tinha um por - te biz - ar - ro, ain - da

ve - jo a sua i - ma - gem no fu - mo do meu cig - arr - o,

ain - da ve - jo a sua imagem no fu - mo do meu cig - arr - o.

A sua al - ma branca e pura hon - es - ta, mod-este e fran - ca, en -

1.

- volv - e a minha al - ma com - o a mor-tal - ha mais bran - ca.

En-volv-e a min-ha al - ma como— a mor-tal-ha mais bran - ca.

2.
abra - ços, co - mo se fos - se en - vol - vi - da na—

— mor - ta - l - ha dos meus osses— do com-o— se foss-e en-vol-vi-

- da na— mort-tal-ha— dos meus osses.

Minha mãe foi cigarreira E tinha um porte bizarro,	*}Repeat*		My mother was a cigarette maker And she had an exotic look,
Ainda vejo a sua imagem No fumo do meu cigarro.	*}Repeat*		I still see her image In the smoke of my cigarette.
A sua alma branca e pura, Honesta, modeste e franca,			Her white and pure soul Honest, modest and sincere,
Envolve a minha alma Como a mortalha mais branca.	*}Repeat*		Wrapped up in my soul Like the whitest shroud.
Coitadinha, já morreu Que o amor de Deus lhe valha,	*}Repeat*		Poor woman, she is now dead, May God's love save her.
Foi com certeza para o Céu, Envolta em branca mortalha.	*}Repeat*		She certainly went to Heaven Wrapped up in a white shroud.
Minha mãe, estrela perdida, Ainda a vejo entre abraços,	*}Repeat*		My mother, a lost star I still see her in my embrace,
Como se fosse envolvida Na mortalha dos meus ossos.	*}Repeat*		As if she were wrapped up In my shroud.

EPILOGUE

ALTHOUGH, AT THE START of this book, I believed I understood how difficult it would be to exclude a great deal of wonderful musical material from this collection, I confess I never fully realised the extent of the problem. It has become increasingly clear that not only a vast number of the finest songs had to be omitted, but also any discussion, or even acknowledgement, of an array of Portugal's most talented singers, writers and musicians. For this transgression I acknowledge sole responsibility, make the deepest apology and humbly beg their forgiveness as well as that of the reader.

It is reasonable to assume that those of you who have read this far had either previously acquired a deep interest in *fado,* or perhaps developed one during this reading. In this regard, it would seem appropriate to say a few words about the future of *fado.*

During my extensive travels in Portugal since the early 1970s I was able to observe the profound changes in the attitudes towards *fado* and its relationship to Portuguese society. On my earliest trips, *fado* could be heard everywhere – sung not only by professionals, but also frequently by talented amateurs, often older men and women with a sprinkling of young workers or college students.

After the Revolution of April 25, 1974, a period of political instability existed during which many people, particularly among the younger element of the population, began to identify *fado* with the past, with the old regime, the days of autocracy, and with the Salazar dictatorship.

In short, they believed *fado* was to be rejected as part of a past they wished to thrust from themselves. They no longer wanted to listen to it or to sing it. This phenomenon was similar to one which occurred about the same time in Argentina, when the younger generation rejected tango, which could thereafter only rarely be found in the Buenos Aires club scene. During this period there was a real fear on the part of lovers of both genres that their future was seriously in doubt. With respect to Portugal, if *fado* was to survive, from where were the future singers to come?

In the past two decades, happily, there has been a profound change for the better in both countries. In Portugal, the younger people have come to realise that *fado,* rather than being identified with any one class or political system, is a deep and vital part of their cultural heritage and that it belongs to all Portuguese.

Recently, with the explosion of music available world-wide through cyber-space and through ever wider distribution of films, CDs and television, greater numbers of non-Portuguese all over the world have become familiar with *fado,* as it is featured ever more widely in concert and on world music radio programmes.

The last 20 years, and particularly the last decade, has seen the emergence of a whole class of new, younger and extremely talented *fadistas,* both men and women. Some have chosen to preserve, and to continue performing, traditional and classic *fado.* Others have elected to reinterpret the old songs, rearranging them, often supplementing the traditional instruments with non-traditional ones. Still others are writing new *fados* or having new ones written for them by some of the finest composers and poets in Portugal. At the time of this writing a partial list of performers carrying *fado,* in all of its forms, to the non-Portuguese speaking world include Margarida Bessa, Dulce Pontes, Mísia, Camané, Mariza, Cristina Branco, Mafalda Arnauth and Teresa Salgeiro.

This phenomenon, of course, sometimes engenders controversy, as it has for generations, as to which new contributions continue to be true *fado* and which do not. And this, probably, is as it should be since *fado* is, thankfully, a living art form and the one essential aspect of life we can all agree on is change.

This book would be presenting a most unfair picture of Lisbon, and in fact, the rest of Portugal, if it conveyed the impression that, while charming and picturesque, it had no modern facilities and was therefore a destination only for the seasoned lover of interesting but arduous, challenging, travel. Nothing could be further from the truth. Lisbon,

Porto, and many of the smaller cities have for many years had excellent facilities, including first-class and deluxe hotels and inns. Portugal had the foresight, many years ago, to establish a chain of excellent government sponsored inns called '*pousadas*', which are often situated in charming historic castles, ·convents and manor houses.

In the last generation, an enormous increase in economic development led to profound changes in all areas of Portuguese society. As a result, the number of luxury hotels, in fact lodging accommodations at all levels, has greatly increased and the historical and other cultural sites made more accessible. The roads and highways are equal to, sometimes superior to, those of Portugal's larger European neighbours. Best of all, unlike some of these neighbours, Portugal has, for the most part, succeeded in retaining the charm, beauty and integrity of its historical and picturesque districts, in spite of these innovations.

In conclusion, it remains only to remind the reader that this book is no more than it appears to be, i.e. a collection of songs. It was never intended to be a scholarly work on the history of *fado*. For those with deeper interest, I refer, particularly the non-Portuguese speakers, to the recent excellent treatise by Paul Vernon, *A History of the Portuguese Fado*, published by Ashgate Press (1998).

I would also be remiss if I did not encourage those with an interest in *fado* to visit the exciting and colourful city of Lisbon and to recommend to those planning such a trip that they visit its magnificent recently opened *fado* museum:

Casa do Fado e da Guitarra Portuguesa (Fado Museum)
Largo do Chafariz de Dentro,
1 Alfama 1100 - 139 Lisboa
Tel: 21 882 34 70 Fax: 21 882 34 78
Closed on Tuesdays
Web site: http://www.egeac.pt/casadofado

FADO HOUSE LOCATIONS

LISTED BELOW are a number of the finest *fado* houses existing in Lisbon at the time this book was completed. It is by no means a complete list and I hope you have the opportunity to search out other fine locations, both old and new. While some of these clubs have been around for many years, restaurants and clubs come and go in Lisbon as anywhere else. These locations were, to my knowledge, existing at the time of writing but please be aware that times and management change. With the more touristy locations, it is wise to arrive later in the evening in order to enjoy the best *fado*.

ADEGA DO MACHADO – Rua do Norte, 91 (Bairro Alto) *ph. 21 346 00 95* Touristy but fun.

ADEGA MESQUITA – In the heart of the Bairro Alto district. Rua Diário de Noticias, 107 *ph. 21 321 92 80*

ADEGA DO RIBATEJO – Rua do Diário de Notícias, 23 (Bairro Alto) *ph. 21 346 83 43* Good *fado*, reasonably priced.

ARCADAS DO FAIA – Rua da Barroca, 54/56 (Bairro Alto) *ph. 21 342 67 42* Good *fado*, fine cuisine, expensive.

CAFÉ LUSO – Travessa da Queimada, 10 (Bairro Alto) *ph. 21 342 22 81* *Fado* only on certain nights. Call first.

CLUB NONO – In the Bairro Alto, Rua do Norte, 7 *ph. 21 342 9989* Authentic *fado*, fine performers.

FADO MAJOR – Largo do Peneireiro, n7 (Alfama) *ph. 21 887 75 08*

GUITARRA DA BICA – Calçada da Bica 13 (Bairro Alto) *ph.21 342 83 09* Authentic *fado*. Inexpensive.

JOÃO DA PRAÇA – Rua S.João da Praça, 92/94 *ph.21 885 27 04* Fine *fado*, fine food, warm, upscale club. This club now also called Restaurante Club do Fado.

MASCOTE DA ATALAIA – Rua da Atalaia, 13 (Bairro Alto) *ph. 21 347 04 08* Authentic *fado*.

O BACALHAO DE MOLHO – Bêco Armazéns Linho, 1 *ph. 21 886 3767* A relatively new *fado* house.

TAVERNA D'EL REY – In the heart of the Alfama, Largo Chafariz de Dentro, 14-15 *ph./fax 21 887 6754*

TAVERNA DO EMBUCADO – Beco de Costumes 10 *ph. 21 886 50 88 / 21 886 50 78* A very popular spot with fine entertainment.

PARREIRINHA DE ALFAMA – Beco do Espirito Santo, 1 (Alfama) *ph. 21 886 02 19 1* Fine, authentic *fado* with excellent food. A favourite spot. Owned by Argentina Santos, one of the last of the great old *fadistas*, who sometimes still performs here.

A SEVERA – Rua das Gáveas, 51 (Bairro Alto) *ph. 21 346 40 06* Touristy, good food.

SENHOR VINHO – Rua do Meio à Lapa, 18 (Lapa) *ph. 21 397 26 81* Only the finest *fadistas* and musicians here. Serves excellent food. Owned by *fadista* star Maria da Fé, who performs along with other fine singers. A favourite.

BIBLIOGRAPHY

ATKINSON, WILLIAM C – *A History of Spain and Portugal* London: Penguin Books, 1960.

BARRETO, MASCARENHAS – *Fado: Origens Líricas e Motivação Poética* Lisboa: Editorial Aster, Lda., (undated).

BIRMINGHAM, DAVID – *A Concise History of Portugal* Cambridge: Cambridge University Press, 1993.

CARVALHO, PINTO DE – *História do Fado* 2nd ed. Lisboa: Publicações D. Quixote, 1984 (Tinop)

TINHORÃO, JOSÉ RAMOS – *Fado: Danca do Brasil, Cantar de Lisboa, O Fim de Um Mito* Lisboa: Editorial Caminho, SA, 1994.

VERNON, PAUL – *A History of the Portuguese Fado*, Aldershot: Ashgate, 1998.

CD TRACK LISTING

1. LISBOA ANTIGA
(Raul Portela / José Galhardo / Amadeu dos Santos)
From the CD *The Art Of Amália*
Artist: Amália Rodrigues

2. COIMBRA
(José Galhardo / Raul Ferrão)
From the CD *The Art Of Amália*
Artist: Amália Rodrigues

3. AI, MOURARIA
(Frederico Valério / Amadeu do Vale)
From the CD *The Art Of Amália*
Artist: Amália Rodrigues

4. POR MORRER UMA ANDORINHA
(Joaquim Frederico de Brito / Francisco Viana / Américo dos Santos)
From the Cassette *Por Morrer Uma Andorinha*
Artist: Carlos do Carmo

5. O EMBUÇADO
(Gabriel d'Oliveira / Alcídia Rodrigues)
From the CD *Biografia do Fado*
Artist: João Ferreira-Rosa

6. A ROSINHA DOS LIMÕES
(Artur Joaquim de Almeida Ribeiro)
Artist: Max

7. VINTE ANOS
(Frederico Valério / Nelson de Barros)
From the Cassette *Celeste Rodrigues: Fados*
Artist: Celeste Rodrigues

8. E FOI-SE A MOCIDADE
(João Nobre Dias / Domingos Gonçalves Costa)
From the Cassette *The Best Of Carlos Ramos (#2)*
Artist: Carlos Ramos

9. MEU BAIRRO ALTO
(Joaquim Frederico de Brito / José Carlos Rocha)
From the Cassette *Sonho Menino*
Artist: Nuno da Câmara Pereira

10. VALEU A PENA
(Moniz Pereira)
From the Cassette *The Best Of Carlos Ramos (#2)*
Artist: Carlos Ramos

11. ROSA ENJEITADA
(José Galhardo / Raul Ferrão)
From the CD *Biografia do Fado*
Artist: Maria Teresa de Noronha

12. FADO HILÁRIO
(Augusto Hilário da Costa Alves)
From the Cassette *Luis Goes*
Artist: Luis Goes

13. DA JANELA DO MEU QUARTO
(António Vilar da Costa / Nóbrega e Sousa)
From the Cassette *Tributo a Tristão da Silva*
Artist: Tristão da Silva

14. A MODA DAS TRANÇAS PRETAS
(Vicente da Câmara / *Fado Ginguinhas*)
From the CD *Biografia do Fado*
Artists: José da Câmara & Don Vicente da Câmara

15. JÚLIA FLORISTA
(Leonel Vilar / Joaquim Pimentel)
From the Cassette *Max e Fado*
Artist: Max

16. O PAGEM
(Alfredo Rodrigues Duarte / Fernando Teles)
From the Cassette *Alfredo Marceneiro*
Artist: Alfredo Marceneiro

17. BONS TEMPOS
(Joaquim Frederico de Brito / José Galhardo)
From the Cassette *Fama-Carlos Ramos-Sempre Que Lisboa Canta*
Artist: Carlos Ramos

18. FADO DA DEFESA
(António Calém / José António Sabrosa)
From the CD *Fado Margarida Bessa*
Artist: Margarida Bessa

19. LISBOA NÃO SEJAS FRANCESA
(José Galhardo / Raul Ferrão)
Artist: Amália Rodrigues

20. HÁ MUITO QUEM CANTE O FADO
(Manuel de Almeida / *Fado Corrido*)
Artist: Manuel de Almeida

21. LISBOA É SEMPRE LISBOA
(Artur Joaquim de Almeida Ribeiro / Nóbrega e Sousa)
Artist: Tristão da Silva

22. FADO TRINTA E UM
(José Maria S. Pereira Coelho / João Alves Coelho)
Artist: António Mello Corrêa

23. TAMANQUINHAS
(Joaquim Frederico de Brito)
Artist: António Mello Corrêa

24. AH, QUANTA MELANCOLIA
(Fernando Pessoa / Alfredo Rodrigo Duarte / *Fado Bailado*)
Artist: Camané

25. MARIA MADALENA
(Gabriel de Oliveira / Augusto Gil / *Fado Mouraria*)
Artist: Lucília do Carmo

26. MINHA MÃE FOI CIGARREIRA
(Filipe de Almeida Pinto / João Linhares Barbosa / Henrique Lopes do Rego / Francisco Duarte Ferreira / *Fado Menor*)
Artist: Filipe Pinto

To remove your CD from the plastic sleeve, lift the small lip on the right to break the perforated flap.
Replace the disc after use for convenient storage.